D1104393

God's Last Metaphor

American Academy of Religion
Studies in Religion

edited by
Conrad Cherry

Number 24

God's Last Metaphor:
The Doctrine of the Trinity
in New England Theology

by Bruce M. Stephens

ATS
231.044
St H

5.44

God's Last Metaphor
The Doctrine of the Trinity
in
New England Theology

Bruce M. Stephens

Scholars Press

17855

6092532

Distributed by
Scholars Press
101 Salem Street
PO Box 2268
Chico, California 95927

God's Last Metaphor:
The Doctrine of the Trinity
in New England Theology

by
Bruce M. Stephens

Copyright © 1981
American Academy of Religion

Library of Congress Cataloging Publication Data

Stephens, Bruce M
    God's last metaphor.
    (Studies in religion ; no. 24 ISSN 0084-6287)
    Includes bibliographical references.
    1. Trinity–History of doctrines. 2. Theology,
Doctrinal–New England–History. I. Title. II. Series:
American Academy of Religion. AAR studies in
religion ; no. 24.

BT109.S69   231'.044'0974   80-11421
ISBN 0-89130-386-3 pbk.

Printed in the United States of America
          1   2   3   4   5
Edward Brothers, Inc.
Ann Arbor, MI. 48104

CONTENTS

PREFACE.. vii

Chapter

1. THE TRINITY AS THE GLORY OF GOD:
    Jonathan Edwards and his Successors.......................1

2. THE TRINITY AS THE ECLIPSE OF GOD:
    The Unitarian Controversy.............................21

3. THE TRINITY AS THE DISTINCTIONS OF GOD:
    Moses Stuart and Samuel Miller.........................35

4. THE TRINITY AS THE LOGIC OF GOD:
    Andrews Norton and Nathaniel W. Taylor.................53

5. THE TRINITY AS THE LANGUAGE OF GOD:
    Horace Bushnell.......................................63

CONCLUSION 75

NOTES 79

PREFACE

The recovery of American religious history has provided us with numerous studies of various aspects of the role of religion in American history. Yet, amidst this recovery it seems to be the case that studies in American religious historiography tend too easily to overlook the centrality of doctrine, thereby neglecting what is a matter of utmost importance. The discussion of religious doctrine was not an idle affair but a consuming interest in which the level of argument ranged from the heights of great intellectual achievement to the depths of acrimonious back-biting. The study of religion in America must seek then to be informed theologically if it is to remain faithful to its task.

In particular, the major figures in the period between Jonathan Edwards and Horace Bushnell deserve to be met within the doctrinal milieu in which they lived and worked. Other studies have explored the anthropological interests of this period by examining the doctrines of original sin and the atonement. The present study is offered as a companion to these and seeks to broaden the discussion by suggesting that the doctrine of the trinity and its Christological implications deserve more systematic treatment than they have heretofore received. Within this somewhat narrow focus the study makes no pretense to be comprehensive, but seeks rather to present a sampler of perspectives upon the trinity. It seems then worthwhile to examine the changes through which the doctrine of the trinity passed, not only to heighten our appreciation for a chapter of religious controversy from the past, but to sensitize us to efforts to understand and state this formidable doctrine in the present.

It is a pleasure to recall the several persons whose suggestions and comments have guided this study, and the institutions where research was conducted. Professor H. Gordon Harland of the University of Manitoba proposed the topic and remained constantly willing to provide encouragement and insight along the way. Dean Bard Thompson of the Graduate School of Drew University shared unselfishly his broad interests in the history of Christian thought, and Professor James Carse of New York University was most helpful with his command of the thought of Jonathan Edwards. I am grateful to my colleague Professor C. Conrad Cherry for the interest and encouragement he has provided; to John D. Vairo, Director of the Delaware County Campus of the Pennsylvania State University, for clearing a path in which research and teaching could go hand in hand; and to Professor James O. Duke, for his judicious advice as associate editor of the American Academy of Religious Series in Religion. A leave during the 1977-78 academic year and grants from the Commonwealth

Campus Scholarly Activity Fund and the Liberal Arts College Central Fund for Research of the Pennsylvania State University made completion of the project possible. The staffs of Rose Memorial Library of Drew University, the Library of Yale Divinity School, and especially Speer Library of Princeton Theological Seminary accorded me every courtesy and conveninece, for which I am grateful. Acknowledgement also is made of permissions granted by *The Princeton Seminary Bulletin* and *Dialog* to print greatly revised and expanded materials which previously appeared as articles in each of these journals.

Finally, what a wife and family endures in the course of such a project is known best only to them, and acknowledgement is made here of the patience and understanding that sustained me during the course of this undertaking.

Bruce M. Stephens

1   The Trinity as the Glory of God

Jonathan Edwards and his Successors

I

Jonathan Edwards died in Princeton, New Jersey, on March 22, 1758, at the age of fifty four, having served but five weeks as the newly elected president of the college in that community. His designs for an epic presentation of *A History of the Work of Redemption* were left unfinished, as were numerous shorter works which were published posthumously. His career as an author began at the age of twelve, when he composed a short essay entitled *Of Insects,* and spanned his years as a student at Yale from 1716-1720, as a pastor to the Northampton, Massachusetts congregation from which he was dismissed after twenty five years of service, and as a missionary to the wilderness settlement of Stockbridge. Whether as a student, under the influence of John Locke, making entries in his notebook on *The Mind,* as a pastor preparing sermons designed to quicken his congregation's awareness of the glory of God, or as a polemicist locked in battle with the Arminians over *The Freedom of the Will,* Edwards's broad intellectual interests were brought to bear upon the theological issues facing eighteenth century New England.

During his lifetime Jonathan Edwards published no separate treatise on the doctrine of the trinity. We have, then, no single work which might stand as a point of departure, as for example his great treatise on *Original Sin.* This lacuna does not necessarily argue that Edwards was indifferent to the doctrine of the trinity or that it played no part in his thought. A careful examination of Edwards's works published during his lifetime and posthumously, as well as the unpublished *Miscellanies,* will reveal the importance of the trinity in his thinking.

Throughout, Edwards approaches the doctrine of the trinity with caution, for it has to do with grand and unfathomable things, against which, however, the mind of man is not rendered useless by its limitations. It is in fact possible for the creature to search for some pattern or rational schema in both creation and redemption, with the knowledge that much will remain hidden and we shall see but "through a glass darkly." There is for man no complete access to the interior of God's triune being, any more than there is complete access to the fulness of His external glory revealed in history. History and trinity both yield meaning only as they are approached by metaphors and figures, as shadows and images in this world reflecting the greater glory of God.

God's great end in both the act of creation and the drama of redemption has a trinitarian structure; indeed, the very form of God's glory or *ad extra* self-communication is trinitarian. In his *Dissertation on the End for Which God Created the World,* Edwards states that "there are many reasons to think that what God has in view, in an increasing communication of himself throughout eternity is an increasing knowledge of God, love of him, and joy in him."[1] The creation offers an opportunity for a glorious display of God's perfections, an *ad extra* communication of *ad intra* knowledge, love, and joy. The inner trinitarian relations of the Godhead or the immanent trinity are reflected in creation and redemption through the economic trinity. The very structure of the divine nature and of human experience are intricated in triune terms; the trinity of knowledge, love, and joy emanate from the will and understanding of God to the will and understanding of man. God's self-revealing, self-communicating act makes use of

> the distinctive faculties of the creature as created in the image of God: even as having these two faculties of understanding and will. God communicated himself to the understanding of the creature in giving him the knowledge of his glory; and to the will of the creature, in giving him holiness, consisting primarily in the love of God: and in giving the creature happiness consisting chiefly in joy in God. These are the sum of that emanation of divine fulness called in Scripture, the glory of God.[2]

Here then is a trinitarian exhibition of God's glory and the reception of it by man, or in Edwards's somewhat neo-Platonic terms, "here is both an emanation and a remanation." Knowledge, love, and joy are relational terms applicable both to the internal being and the external act of God. There is a correspondence between the ontological structure of creation and the internal life of God, just as there is a correspondence between the historical structure of redemption and the internal life of God.

For Edwards the doctrine of the trinity is not the product of detached and abstract thinking, but grows out of the relational experiences which are at the heart of faith. This concreteness lends to his understanding of the trinity a certain practicality which was lost in subsequent New England theology and recovered only much later. The trinity bestows richness and life to the plentitude of God's being and act and, in turn, brings vitality to man's capacity to receive and respond to revelation as a creature of understanding and will. To know, to love, and to enjoy God is God's chief end for man in creation. To this end, God has made His glory fully visible, clothing Himself in the things of nature and history.

The trinity is man's assurance that God Himself is not something different from God in revelation. God is not "wholly other," for the *ad intra* and the *ad extra* relation of the Godhead are triune. What God is and what God does have a triune structure imaged in the soul of man, so that the structure of the self as a creature of understanding and will becomes a clue to the nature of the triune God. "There is yet more of an image of the Trinity in the soul of man. There is the mind and its understanding or idea, and the will or affection, or love: answering to God, the idea of God and the love of God.''[3] Needless to say, the interior life of the Godhead is not open to careful inspection and exhaustive description, and the direction Edwards takes is distinctly away from the abstract and toward the concrete, moving from experience to reflection *via* doctrine. Edwards, therefore, found in the doctrine of the trinity a means both to preserve the integrity of the self and to speak intelligibly of God's being in the world as well as beyond it. The trinity encompasses both time and eternity, the immanent and the transcendent.

Thus the tension of beyondness and relatedness is maintained in Edwards's thought through the emanation and remanation of divine glory by which the three summary perfections of knowledge, love, and joy are both exhibited by God and acknowledged by man.

> This twofold way of the Deity's flowing forth *ad extra*, answers to the twofold way of the Deity's proceeding *ad intra*, the proceeding and generation of the Son, and the proceeding and breathing forth of the Holy Spirit; and indeed is only a kind of second proceeding of the same persons, their going forth *ad extra*, as before they proceed *ad intra*.''[4]

There are distinct parallels here with Augustine in the analogy for the trinity which Edwards draws from the human mind's knowing and loving itself. The trinitarian structure of the being of God and the psychological structure of man go hand in hand. God's disposition to know and love Himself in the second and third persons of the trinity is a communication of His excellence and beauty. And this is "a disposition in God, as an original property of his nature, and an emanation of his own infinite fulness, and was what excited him to create the world; and so that the emanation itself was aimed at by him as a last end of creation.''[5] Through the trinity, God becomes the highest truth, and most apparent good, and the greatest joy for man as an understanding and willing creature.

We have noted that Edwards did not publish a separate essay or treatise on the trinity during his lifetime. However, among the papers of Edwards A. Park was found a manuscript of Edwards's on the trinity, which subsequently was edited by George P. Fisher and published on the occasion of the 200th anniversary of the author's birth under the title *An Unpublished Essay of Edwards on the Trinity*. The *Essay* provides a transition into the trinitarian nature of redemption, but it must be treated with some care. Since the entries were made over a long period of time, it is not clear that Edwards intended the work for publication, even though, as its editor observes, "it is the most comprehensive and complete discussion of the doctrine on all sides that has emanated from its author.''[6]

The *Essay* is determined to establish, among other things, the eternity of the inner-trinitarian relations and the fact that the trinity is not an *ad hoc* arrangement that goes into effect only at the moment of the incarnation.

God has had a "most perfect idea of Himself" from eternity. The second person of the trinity is "the Eternal, necessary, Perfect, Substantial and Personal Idea which God hath of himself."[7] God's idea of Himself differs from human ideas in that it is not only ideal, but substantial and personal. Christ is most properly, as the second person of the trinity, the eternal divine nature and essence repeated in time. The trinity of persons is completed by the procession of the Spirit as the bond of union between the first and second perons, in which and through which

> the Deity becomes all act, the divine essence itself flows out and tis as it were breathed forth in love and Joy. So that the Godhead therein stands forth in yet another manner of subsistence, and there Proceeds the 3rd Person in the Trinity, the holy spirit, viz., the Deity in act, for there is no other act but the act of the will.[8]

There are, then, real distinctions in the Godhead which consist of God, His idea of Himself, His love and delight in Himself. The following passage makes clear Edwards's understanding of these personal distinctions in the Godhead:

> The Son is the deity generated by Gods understanding, or having an Idea of himself & subsisting in that Idea. The Holy Gh. is the Deity subsisting in act, or the divine essence flowing out and Breathed forth in Gods Infinite love to & delight in himself. & I believe the whole divine Essence does Truly & distinctly subsist both in the divine Idea & divine Love, and that each of them are Properly distinct Persons. It confirms me in it that this is the True Trinity because Reason is sufficient to tell us that there must be these distinctions in the deity, viz., of G. (absolutely considered), & the Idea of G., & Love & delight, & there are no other Real distinctions in G. that can be thought. There are but these three distinct Real things in G. Whatsoever else can be mentioned in G. are nothing but meer modes or Relations of Existence.[9]

Apart from Scripture, "reason is sufficient" to establish the real distinctions in the trinity. The problem is to maintain both the oneness and threeness, and Edwards is faced here with an issue which from its earliest statement has plagued the doctrine of the trinity.

But the doctrine of the trinity is not a matter of reason alone, and Edwards does not allow it to become unhinged from the historical drama of redemption, for the relation of God and the history of redemption is focused in the trinity. The dramatic encounter of sinful man with a redeeming God does not take place abstractly, but in time and in the soul of man; therefore, the language of the trinity is relational, personal, and experiential. Man's business is with God, and he is created with the capability of communing with God through his understanding and his will. The trinity is therefore the *locus* for knowing and speaking about God and man—indeed, the whole of reality is understood in terms of the trinity.

The relation of the trinity to the drama of redemption is more explicitly treated in a posthumously published essay entitled *Observations*

Concerning the Scripture Oeconomy of the Trinity and Covenant of Redemption. It was this essay to which Horace Bushnell called attention in the Preface to his *Christ in Theology* in 1851, causing quite a stir among the defenders and detractors of Edwards. Bushnell complained that he had been denied access to the manuscript on the grounds of the nature of its contents, and the rumor was afloat that Edwards had penned an *a-priori* argument for the Trinity. Oliver Wendell Holmes rather smugly claimed, "Edward's views appear to have undergone a great change in the direction of Arianism, or of Sabellianism, which is an old-fashioned Unitarianism, or at any rate show a defection from his former standard of orthodoxy."[10] Meanwhile, at Andover Seminary, the patrons of the orthodox *Bibliotheca Sacra* were busy preparing a defense of Edwards assuring their readers that "the popular rumors regarding President Edwards changes of theological opinion are many of them utterly false, many of them singularly exaggerated, and all unreliable."[11]

The *Observations* were edited by E. C. Smyth from Edwards's *Miscellanies* (especially No. 1062), and delineate the "oeconomy" of God's self-communication in redemption. There is accordingly "an order of acting fit to the order of subsisting," and again it is the trinity which gives structure to both. Edwards's inheritance of a Puritan penchant for order seems to be answered by the doctrine of the trinity. This doctrine gives coherence and richness to the being of God in eternity and to the action of God in time. The persons of the Godhead

> have as it were formed themselves into a society, for carrying on the great design of glorifying the diety and communicating its fulness, in which is established a certain oeconomy and order of acting. . .There is a natural decency and fitness in that order and oeconomy that is established.[12]

Further, there is

> a subordination of the Persons of the Trinity in their actings with respect to the creature. . .and particularly in what they act in the affairs of man's redemption. . . . However it is very manifest that the Persons of the Trinity are not inferior to one another in glory and excellency of nature.[13]

Just as God's chief end in the creation of the world bears a trinitarian pattern, the image or shadow of which is in the soul of man, so now in the redemption of the world there is a covenant which proceeds according to a trinitarian pattern.

Perhaps no single concept was used more in Puritan theology to bring the glory of an inscrutable God into relationship with sinful man than that of the covenant. This theme is taken into and becomes a constitutive element in Edwards's appropriation of the Christian trinity. The covenant of redemption becomes "a particular excellent method" for God to communicate Himself to man. This *ad extra* movement of God to man is grounded in the *ad intra* relations of the Godhead, and

> we must distinguish between the covenant of redemption, that is an establishment of wisdom wonderfully contriving a particular method for the most conveniently obtaining a great end, and that establishment that is founded in fitness and decency and the natural order of the eternal and necessary subsistence of the Persons of the Trinity. [14]

The idea of the covenant is grounded in the doctrine of the trinity, and rather than abandoning covenant theology, Edwards sought to restore its trinitarian base.

The determination to redeem mankind is a decision arrived at by the Father and the Son (excluding the Spirit) on the basis of the trinitarian status and dignity of each. The work of redemption represents the consent of the Son to treatment far different than that of the immanent trinity, for in the economic trinity the Son is subjected to suffering and humiliation in His office as Redeemer. The important thing to note is that the immanent trinity persists before the covenant of redemption is conceived, during its execution, and following its consummation. Just as the trinity did not come into existence at creation, neither is it established by redemption—it is the presupposition of both. Against Sabellianism, Edwards is asserting that it is not the trinity but the covenant of redemption that goes into effect with the incarnation. Against Arianism, he is asserting that the second person of the trinity is not a product of the Father's will, and therefore essentially subordinate, but He is of necessity the Son and therefore equal with the Father. It is the covenant of redemption that is a matter not of necessity but of God's willing to redeem man. The Sonship of Christ, however, is a matter of necessity and not of will.

This distinction is important in terms of the Christological implications of the trinity, especially as expressed in the doctrine of the eternal Sonship of Christ. Edwards refuses to divorce his Christology from the doctrine of the trinity. He rejects the idea that

> the Sonship of the second Person in the trinity consists only in the relation He bears to the Father in His mediatorial character; and that His generation or proceeding from the Father as *a Son*, consists only in His being appointed, constituted and authorized of the Father to the office of a mediator; and that there is no other priority of the Father to the Son but that which is voluntarily established in the covenant of redemption. [15]

The eternal Sonship of Christ is here maintained as an essential concomitant of the trinity, both to protect the deity of Christ and to avoid modalism.

The trinity is at the heart of both Edwards's idea of the covenant and his Christology and is not allowed therefore to drift into some obscure corner of his thought. The unity and distinctions of the Godhead, on the one hand, and the humanity and divinity of Christ, on the other, are at stake in a proper statement of the trinity. The distinctions in the Godhead are eternal, necessary, and essential. Even apart from the covenant of redemption, God is triune. So, too, the Sonship of Christ is not a product of time, but established in eternity.

The nature and work of the Holy Spirit are more fully outlined in Edwards's *Treatise on Grace*, published in Scotland by Alexander Grosart in 1865. Here the role of the Spirit as related to the inner-trinitarian life of the Godhead, on the one hand, and to the spiritual life of man, on the other, is clarified. It is the personal agency of the third person of the trinity which bestows to the soul "relish of the supreme excellency of the Divine nature, inclining the heart to God as the chief good."[16] This breathing forth of the divine essence and the indwelling of the Spirit in the heart of man gives a taste of the sweetness of things divine, and "is in a peculiar manner called by the name of love."[17] The love of the Father for the Son, the bond of union between the first and second persons, is the Holy Spirit. Again, the Spirit proceeds in eternity between the Father and the Son, and in time between God and the affections of man. The procession of the Spirit, no less than the generation of the Son, is an eternal mystery, and although confident that human reason is capable of exploring the trinity to some degree, Edwards has a profound sense of the mysterious nature of the subject and the limits of reason in dealing with it. Reason must be accompanied by Scripture, and in concert reason and Scripture together testify to the necessity of a trinity.

God, according to Edwards, reflects upon Himself and takes delight in what He sees, "so that if we turn in all ways in the world, we shall never be able to make more than these three: God, the idea of God, and delight in God."[18] These are the only real distinctions that the light of reason and the revelation of Scripture will admit to in the Godhead. The empirical ground of this claim is the conviction that "the Almighty's knowledge is not so different from ours, but that ours is the image of it."[19] We are told elsewhere that "of all the beings that we see or know anything of, man's soul only seems to be the image of that supreme universal principle."[20] This comment is not to suggest, though, that the analogy between the soul of man and the being of God is perfect or that the mystery of the glorious trinity is to be laid bare by the powers of human reason and the use of psychological analogies. It suggests only that man bears the image of the trinity as a shadow of divine things. The analogy is imperfect because when God thinks, the idea He has of Himself is immediate and actual, substantial and perfect—the Logos. Man's thinking produces external signs rather than the thing itself and is therefore imperfect.[21] However, God frequently chooses imperfect things as shadows of the perfect and most excellent.[22]

The relational terms of love, knowledge, and joy are central to Edwards's trinitarian formulations, and when these are jettisoned, the

doctrine of the trinity tends toward a logical syllogism unable to touch
either the understanding or the affections of man. To Edwards the understanding is a relational faculty, a mode of relating to reality involving the
whole self: it is a participatory understanding. The understanding is active,
it participates in perception, it is man's link with Being.[23] The will also is a
mode of relation to reality involving the whole self. The direction of the will
is determinative, for the self becomes what it identifies as the greatest apparent good. The distinctions in man then, are as real as the distinctions in
God, and they are three in number: "Namely, the spirit itself, and its understanding, and its will or inclination or love. And this indeed is all the real
distinction there is in created spirits."[24]

Finally, however, Edwards's adumbration of the doctrine of the trinity
is not primarily an argument for its reasonableness, nor is it a lofty flight of
the mind. It is rather a search for pattern, a quest for design, in order better
to understand the nature of a self-communicating God who makes Himself
visible to His creatures through His triune being and act. There is an
economy or fitness in the way God does things; He does not act arbitrarily,
blundering His way through time and eternity by spur of the moment deci-
sions. There is an order, an underlying design, a providential economy in
creation and redemption. The trinity, then, is no instrumental device
created as a make-shift design to redeem a creation that has gone astray. It
is not some sudden storm of divine wisdom that went into effect two
thousand years ago. The task, then, is to catch something of the grandeur of
design, the size of the ledger, on which Edwards is writing his score. The
theme throughout, from the opening strains to the thunderous finale, is the
glory of God, upon which creation and redemption are variations. The
trinity is the ledger, that which provides the undergirding structure for the
whole, even though it is not fore-front in Edwards's work. The embellish-
ments are provided by the eternal Sonship of Christ and the eternal procession of the Spirit as the wisdom and love of God, respectively. Beauty and
excellence mark the symphonic whole, bearing witness to the glory of God
and "a new sense of things." The trinity is finally not a doctrine but an
experience, "a sense of the heart," that man is to glorify God and enjoy
Him forever.

II

The legacy of Jonathan Edwards to American religious life and
thought has been assessed from a variety of perspectives and the verdicts
range across a wide spectrum. Few deny, however, that Edwards is a major
religious thinker, and one of the problems of American religious historiography is getting through and beyond him. The forces leading to Edwards
have been traced with some care, but the lines leading away from him have
not received the attention they deserve. Beyond the anthropological issues

ussion. It is possible, and Edwards is a case in point, to have a
ian theology without a conscious explication of the trinity, and
y too operates out of an unexamined Reformed trinitarian bias. The
on becomes what happens when the doctrine of the trinity specifically
under attack, as it did in New England. To withstand the attacks
d against it, the doctrine of the trinity needed something more than
direct presence in theology. Simply to assert that the trinity must be
ed in order to understand the gospel was unconvincing to many for
this doctrine became increasingly open to question. Bellamy's trinity
t simply could not withstand the inroads of the age of reason. That
should occur against a doctrine declared to be incomprehensible
d come as no surprise: it was inevitable.

f the doctrine of the trinity *per se* is not of immediate interest to
my, the soteriological function of each person of the trinity is of
rtance to him.

> That there are three persons in the Godhead and yet but one God, we must believe;
> and what characters they sustain, and what parts they act in the affair of our salva-
> tion, we must understand. . . .Not how they are three persons and yet but one God,
> the manner of which is not needful to be known; but the offices and characters
> they sustain and the different parts they act in the great affair of saving sinners.[28]

divine unity becomes somewhat obscured behind an emphasis on the
eness, for the focus of Bellamy's interest in the trinity is on the suitable-
s of each person to its part in the drama of redemption. Thus, according
Bellamy,

> The Father sustains the character of supreme Lord and Governor, asserts the rights
> of the Godhead, maintains the honour of his law and government. The Son becomes
> mediator between God and man, to open a door for God to show mercy to man
> consistently with his honour, and for man to return to God with safety. The Holy
> Spirit is the Sanctifier, to work in sinners to will and to do, and recover and bring
> them to repent and return to God, through Jesus Christ.[29]

he tendency toward modalism here is understandable in the light of the
verall structure of Bellamy's theology around the themes of law and
ospel. If "true religion" is to be ordered around these twin poles, the
rinity is thereby made instrumental to the exercises of God's judgment and
mercy. The focus, therefore, quite naturally falls on the trinity of manifest-
ation, and the immanent trintiy is declared incomprehensible. The author is
under no compulsion to develop the doctrine of the trinity in itself; it is
simply one of the givens of revelation which, quite apart from our ability to
comprehend it, is to be believed. As we have seen, Edwards exhibited considerably more confidence in the ability of reason to explore the mystery of
the trinity.

of original sin and atonement, each of which has ↑
other major doctrinal developments, including the
The immediate task is to examine selected immedia↑
and to follow the course of the development in the
with special attention given to its Christological imp

   Among those who studed theology with Edwa↑
parsonage was Joseph Bellamy (1719-1790), who
brightest students and destined to become his most lc
uate of Yale in 1735 at the age of sixteen, Bellamy
Edwards before accepting a call to the Bethlem, Con
where he was to remain for his lifetime. Bellamy devo
toral duties in this backwoods parish and pursued tl
rigorously and relentlessly. To some he seemed overbe
censorious, while to many he was a brilliant conversa
the most commanding figures of the New England pul↑
as a preacher ranked second only to the venerable G
good eighteenth century fashion, Bellamy boarded th↑
the Bethlem parsonage, some of whom were attracted
techniques, while others soon departed because of hi↑
figure of international reputation (he received a D.D. ↑
of Aberdeen in 1768), Bellamy was a loyal and fer↑
prayers for the success of the colonial arms were offered ↑
heavenly grace with frequent urgency. He enjoyed the c
his ministerial colleague, Jonathan Edwards, with whom
changed books and dickered in livestock.

   The most widely read of his works was *True Rel↑*
which ranks second only to Edwards's *Religious Affectio*
tion into the nature of experimental religion. In a Pr↑
Edwards, the work receives a hearty endorsement as a "↑
discourse, and well it might, for the book throughout ↑
Edwards, although not slavishly dependent upon him. The ↑
the trinity in "true religion" is for the most part left unclea↑
tents himself with a traditional statement of the trinity, choc
low some of Edwards's more suggestive manuscripts to
access. He asserts, in good Reformed tradition, that the ↑
trinity is the interpretive principle of theology: "Right app
God help us to understand the Law, and right apprehensions
will help us to understand the Gospel."[27] But as for what th↑
itself, Bellamy accepts the Westminster Confession without fu↑
tion or explanation. He is aware that among the items in
system of divinity is the doctrine of the trinity, and he affirms
an item of orthodoxy but does not develop the doctrine as a m↑
importance in itself. By and large, the trinity is presented as som
believed rather than understood, as incomprehensible and there↑

In *A Treatise on the Divinity of Christ,* Bellamy reaffirms his basic position on the doctrine of the trinity and turns to establishing the deity of Christ and the nature of Sonship. Bellamy seeks to establish the divinity of Christ by grounding His existence antecedent to the incarnation, in the trinity. Again, however, he refuses to probe this inner-trinitarian relationship on the grounds that the trinity defies understanding and invites rather simple belief.

> I say, when we observe these representations in the sacred records, it becomes evident that Father, Son and Holy Ghost, although they are but one God (I Jn. 5:7) plainly act as though they were *three distinct persons.* And if our reason cannot find out how they are *three,* and yet but *one*; and if God has not thought it needful to instruct us in this point; yet so far as is revealed, so far may we believe; and that with a faith sufficiently distinct to lay a foundation for practice.[30]

As to the Sonship of Christ, essentially there are two Sonships—one in eternity and one in time. As the Son of God in His divine nature, Christ has an eternal relation to the Father as the second person of the trinity. As the Son of David in His human nature, Christ takes on the form of a servant in time. "Christ is the form of God. . .plainly before He took upon Him the form of a servant: before He appeared in the likeness of man; i.e., before His incarnation." However, in order to prepare for the gospel and to ready man for Christ's appearance as a servant, through a long period of "three or four thousand years" God "appointed Him such works to do. . .as might effectually determine His true character."[31] This scheme of an eternal and temporal Sonship was to recur in New England theology as a method of delineating the two natures of Christ.

Although we lack a specific treatise from Bellamy on the trinity, it is clear that this doctrine is accorded considerable respect, at least from a distance. Bellamy is convinced that "the sum and substance of the gospel may be reduced to two or three points, which must be in a manner self-evident to a mind rightly disposed."[32] Among these two or three points is, of course, the doctrine of the trinity: "for as all Christians were baptized in the name of the Father and of the Son and of the Holy Ghost; so right apprehension of the character and offices of these three, is the sum of all Christian knowledge."[33] The trinity is among the great doctrines of the gospel that are not open to dispute. It is simply part of the faith once delivered to the saints and is therefore to be believed. As "moral governor" of the world, God reveals Himself to man in such a manner that His law is honored and man is saved. The instrument best designed to accomplish this objective is the trinity. In short, it is the atonement that has the prior interest in Bellamy's thought, while the trinity is simply affirmed as an item of orthodox faith without any further inquiry. The overall emphasis is upon the threeness of the Godhead in the work of redemption and the moral government of God, with a subsequent neglect of the unity of the Godhead and the internal relations of the trinity. There is, however, good historical precedence for this, as the same strain may be found in Origen, Basil, and the Gregorys, not to speak of Edwards himself.

III

When the time came for New England theology to consolidate some of its gains and losses into a system of theology, it was Samuel Hopkins's (1721-1803) *System of Doctrines* that sought to bring order out of chaos. Hopkins's impact on American religious life and thought has only recently received the attention it is due.[34] As humanitarian, theologian, and for many years pastor of the church in Newport, Rhode Island, Hopkins exerted a powerful influence through his writings. Like Bellamy, Hopkins was a student of Edwards's in the Northampton manse, where he arrived in 1741, despondent about the genuineness of his Christian life. Despite the best efforts of Edwards's wife Sarah to comfort and assure the young theological student who would make her home his sometime residence for two years, Hopkins persisted in his state of spiritual uncertainty throughout the parish round in which he assisted his tutor. His fear of self-deception regarding the state of his soul was never completely overcome, but under the watchful eye of his teacher he progressed both in his spiritual life and in his theological studies, and he received ordination from the congregation at Great Barrington, Massachusetts, in December, 1743. Needless to say, a wife of frail health and his eight children heightened his sensitivity to cares of the world, especially in light of the always meager pecuniary returns his pastoral efforts brought.

These worldly cares were offset somewhat by the constant theological companionship of both Bellamy and Edwards. When the latter was dismissed from his pulpit in Northampton, it was Hopkins who was instrumental in procuring the Stockbridge call for him. Always one to seek the comforts of the mind rather than those of the body, Hopkins spent fourteen hours a day in his study pursuing the truth as he saw it and defending it with all the rigor of his mental energies. His thorough-going patriotism during the Revolution earned him the opposition of the Tories, on the one hand, while his "Hopkinsian" independence of thought earned him the opposition of the Old Calvinists, on the other. The result was dismissal from the Great Barrington parish and removal to the bustling seaport town of Newport, Rhode Island, where he was to survive war, criticism for his opposition to the slave trade, and continued pecuniary hardship for thirty-three years. Hopkins was far from a recluse who spun his theological system indifferent to the benevolence of God and the greatest good of his fellow man. He fell heir to Edwards's manuscripts, and the influence of his tutor and friend was immense, although again, as with Bellamy, it is evident that Hopkins moves with considerable independence and originality in his *System of Doctrines.*

According to Hopkins, "a system of divinity is as proper and important as a system of jurisprudence, physic, or natural philosophy."[35] The "system" is arranged around the Westminster Confession and thus in what is essentially a trinitarian scheme. While Edwards made much of God's self-contemplation and His delight in this contemplation, Hopkins chose not to entangle himself in any analogical derivations of the trinity, but rested content with a traditional restatement of Nicaea *via* the Westminster Confession. The unity of God is pressed strongly, on the grounds that evidence from revelation and reason argue for it. To dislodge the unity of God is not only absurd, but an evil and "the worst sort of atheism."

However, according to the evidence not of reason but of revelation, there are three distinct subsistencies or "persons" in this one God. The witness of Scripture is to a trinity of persons, clearly seen in the Old Testament where the Hebrew word for God is plural, and from such evidence as the ancient address, "Holy, Holy, Holy," which is a clear reference to the trinity. In the New Testament, there is overt evidence for the doctrine of the trinity in the baptismal formula, and even one reference to the trinity of the Godhead is enough to confirm that this is a doctrine of truth revealed to men.

Although the trinity is an essential doctrine of the *System,* Hopkins chooses to treat it very cautiously and sparingly, not wishing to let slip any statement he might later regret. He simply notes that the term "person" in the context of trinitarian thought "does not import the same distinction which is expressed by it when applied to men. It means nothing inconsistent with the highest perfection, or with these three being really and most perfectly *one* God."[36] Though not enthusiastic about the use of the term persons, there is none better and "it is not pretended that this word, when used in this instance, can be so defined as to give any clear and adequate idea of a subject so mysterious and infinitely incomprehensible."[37]

Refusing to probe at any length the *ad intra* nature and relations of the Godhead, Hopkins rests content merely to assert that "this [triune] distinction and manner of existence is peculiar and essential to the infinite eternal Being as the most perfect, happy and glorious mode of existence, independent of any divine operations *ad extra*, and the proper foundation of these. . . ."[38] This is as far as Hopkins will go, and theological students who fed on the *System of Doctrines* for several decades would simply have to be content that our not being able to comprehend the trinity is no reason why we should not believe it as revealed. Since "God exists in a manner infinitely above our reason," we should not despair of our ignorance but simply believe the truths of the system. Again, there were increasing numbers for whom this invitation to revel in the incomprehensible simply was not at all attractive.

While Hopkins accepts as a revealed truth that God is triune *ad intra*, it is the *ad extra* operations that interest him, for the trinity becomes the occasion or the mode through which God exercises His benevolence. The trinity is essential, for "without this distinction in God, there would have been no foundation or sufficiency in Him for the exercise of mercy. . . ."[39] These distinctions enable God to go outside Himself to satisfy the demands of justice. The trinity is the framework within which God satisfies the demands of His justice and exercises mercy toward His creatures. The interest is more in the relation of mercy and justice (the atonement) and less in the becoming flesh of the Godhead (the incarnation). Thus, Hopkins may safely assert that the trinity is "an important and essential doctrine of Christianity," yet he feels under no compulsion to conduct an elaborate inquiry into the doctrine. In fact, he despairs that many attempts to explain it have only darkened counsel and given advantage to its opponents. It is almost with a sigh of relief that his *System* passes on to consider other matters, content that at least by mention of the trinity the requirements of theological system building had been met.

This is not to suggest that Hopkins did not consider himself a thoroughly trinitarian thinker. A brief examination of the Christological implications of the trinity in his thought will reveal the importance of the doctrine of the trinity to him. The question centers around the Sonship of Christ, a subject upon which Hopkins was considerably exercised, as the amount of space given to the topic in his *System of Doctrines* indicates. Again, the point of departure is the covenent of redemption by which "God in a Trinity of persons, gives Himself to the redeemed as their infinite, everlasting portion and happiness."[40] The task is to guard the personhood of a Redeemer equal to the work of redemption, while at the same time preserving the two natures of Christ as truly human and truly divine. There is an internal covenant of redemption among the persons of the trinity which determines that man is to be saved and by which the part that each person is to play in the work of redemption is fixed and voluntarily undertaken. There is also a covenant of grace, between the persons of the trinity and believers, a covenant fit, formed and suited to the state and circumstances of man. This external covenant of redemption reveals the operation of the Godhead in time.

Hopkins argues first against those who hold the doctrine of the preexistence of Christ's human soul. He expands upon Edwards's "Reasons against Dr. Watt's Notion of the Pre-Existence of Christ's Human Soul," by asserting that "the human nature of Christ began to exist when it was conceived in the Virgin Mary, and not before."[41] Making a high and exalted creature out of Christ by attributing to Him a pre-existent human soul distorts His existence from eternity as the second person of the blessed trinity. Hopkins charges that the notion of the pre-existence of Christ's human soul is a useless and unreasonable idea designed to deny the divinity of Christ. It in a measure at least, obscures and weakens the doctrine of the divinity of Christ, and that of a Trinity of persons in the Deity. . . . since many, if not most of those who have embraced this sentiment of the pre-existence of the human nature of the Redeemer give up the doctrine of the Trinity, of three distinct persons subsisting eternally in one God, independent of his works, or manner of operation. . . .[42]

Interestingly, Hopkins's defense of the doctrine of the trinity comes not when he is specifically dealing with it in the outline of his system, but when he is brought to consider its Christological implications.

Hopkins was sensitive to the rise of Arianism in New England and sought to hold the line against those who were "rather inclined to consider this first and greatest creature as a divine person, by a peculiar union to Deity or to God; not considering Him as subsisting in three persons, or as in any sense three, considered in Himself; but only in his different manner of acting, and distinct offices in his relation to his creatures, and works respecting them."[43] This fear of New England Arianism in turn leads him into an attempt to set the record straight regarding the history of the doctrine of the eternal Sonship of Christ, not only in New England but within the broader stream of church history. If the humanity of Christ is linked to the incarnation, the divinity of Christ is linked to the trinity through which He is the bearer of an eternal Sonship. Noting that trini-tarians in general subscribe to the teaching of eternal Sonship, "not all are agreed as to the foundation of his Sonship and in what it consists." Hopkins observes:

it has been generally believed, and the common doctrine of the church of Christ, from the beginning of the fourth century, and so far as appears from the days of the apostles to this time, that Jesus Christ is the *eternal* Son of God; that his Sonship is essential to him, as the second person in the Trinity, and that in this sense he is the only begotten Son of the Father, intercedent to his incarnation and independent on it, even for eternity. But there are some who think that the Sonship of the Redeemer consists in an union of the second person of the Trinity or the Word, with the human nature; and that he became the Son of God by becoming man; and therefore before the incarnation there was no Son of God; though there were a trinity of persons in the Godhead. This opinion seems to be rather gaining ground, and spreading of late.[44]

This is probably as clear a statement of the problem as New England theology will offer, and it is no small credit to Hopkins's perceptive mind that he discerned the direction of the New England tradition and warned against its failure properly to sustain what he saw to be the vital link between the doctrine of the trinity and Christology, i.e., the eternal Sonship of Christ. George Park Fisher, student and critic of New England theology, observed that "with the expiration of the century in which Edwards lived, the Nicene doctrine of the eternal generation of the Son ceased to exist any longer as a part of New England orthodoxy."[45] However, Hopkins discerned that the question of the eternal Sonship of Christ was "a question respecting the character of the Redeemer, therefore it is important." Jesus Christ did not become the Son of God by becoming man; rather, the attribute of Sonship belongs to Him antecedent to the incarnation. This question of the filiation of the Son was important to Hopkins in his polemics against not only Arianism, but also against Sabellianism, "which considers the Deity as but one person, and to be three only out of respect to the different manner or kind of his operation."[46] The distinctions in the Godhead denoted by the term "persons" are real and eternal.

Hopkins consoled his readers and his theological students that if all of this is somewhat incomprehensible and mysterious, that is only as it should be. God acts in mysterious ways, the being and mode of His existence are infinitely above our comprehension. Since the eternal generation of the Son is a divine generation for which there are no human analogies, it must necessarily remain a mystery, even as the trinity itself is finally a mystery. But, taken together, these two doctrines are the means best suited to the minds and hearts of men for God to convey ideas of Himself to them, and to accomplish His redemptive purposes for them. The issue at stake is a right understanding of the character of the Redeemer and of the work of redemption. "Those who exclude the trinity exclude the possibility of redemption and of a Redeemer equal to the work. Had there not been a God subsisting in three persons, so distinct as to covenant with each other and act a separate and distinct part in the work of redemption, man could not have been redeemed, and there could have been no Redeemer."[47] If Samuel Hopkins made no bold contributions to the doctrine of the trinity *per se*, it does become clear in the course of his *System of Doctrines* that the trinity is important to his understanding and explication of the Christian faith, and, further, that Hopkins is an important figure in the development of American religious thought.

IV

Our treatment of New England theologians can by no means be complete, but the inclusion of Nathaniel Emmons (1745-1840) is dictated by the impact he made during the course of his sixty-four year reign over the Franklin, Massachusetts, parish.[48] Emmon's theological education consisted of a Yale diploma and two years itinerant study with various ministers. His weak voice and unimposing pulpit manner militated against a call until the Franklin parish summoned him in 1773, a post in which he outlived three wives and most of his fifteen children. His life was one of rigorously disciplined long hours in his study preparing sermons, which, when collected, were published as seven volumes of *Works*. Under no circumstance would Emmons submit to manual labor, and hay would rot in the field before he would consent to help make it. His habit of tobacco chewing, his manner of dress, and his adherence to passing customs made this divine a rather interesting spectacle in his old age. For the most part, his life was confined to his study, where he wore thin the planks in the flooring beneath his desk, thinking his way through the Christian faith, and spinning the web of truth as he saw it.

For Emmons, theology is derived from a few fundamental facts or principles. Truth is presented as facts, from which all else follows. Accordingly, "the gospel is built upon a number of essential doctrines which constitute its nature and distinguish it from every other scheme of religion."[49] Christianity, then, consists of a scheme of fundamental principles derived by reason and delivered to faith. "To deny these doctrines is to deny the gospel. To deny the first principles of the system is to deny the system."[50] Obviously, the trinity is a fact or a first principle of the Christian system, an undeniable truth of faith. "The gospel is so absolutely and obviously founded on the doctrine of three persons in one God, that whoever denies this great and fundamental truth must, in order to be consistent, deny all the peculiarities which distinguish revealed from natural religion."[51]

Disdaining any attempts to probe the inner-trinitarian nature and relations of the Godhead, Emmons will say only that there is a certain "something" in the divine nature which lays a proper foundation for personal distinctions, but all human analogies to this something break down, and he refuses to elaborate further on it. He will not venture a psychological analogy, and he complains about the dangers of over-curious speculation of theologians on the trinity. It is rather to the covenant of redemption that Emmons turns in dealing with the doctrine of the trinity, convinced that the trinity has its roots here. The distinctions in the Godhead "clearly appear to originate from the work of redemption, and probably were unknown in heaven until the purposes of grace were there revealed."[52] With respect to the great work of redemption, there is an economy of personalities whereby each person of the trinity fulfills a peculiar office as Creator, Mediator, or Sanctifier. The purpose of redemption is to make God known in all His perfections and His whole character—which is three in respect to personality, but one in respect to essence.

The result is an emphasis not upon the unity but upon the distinctions of the Godhead, not upon oneness but upon threeness. Accordingly, "Christians ought to exercise affections towards God corresponding to this personal distinction in his peculiar mode of existence."

To the Father, the first person in the trinity, for his love to them in providing a Saviour for them. . . .This great and distinguishing expression of the Father's love to them, lays them under distinct obligation to feel and express peculiar gratitude to Him, as the prime mover and actor in promoting their eternal salvation. In the second place, they ought to gratefully acknowledge the astonishing grace of the Lord Jesus Christ, the second person in the adorable trinity, in what he has done to atone for their sins and open the door of mercy to them. . . .Christians are under the strongest and most endearing obligations to feel and express the warmest gratitude

to Christ in particular, for what he has done and suffered in his mediatorial character, to save them from the wrath to come and make them happy forever. In the
third place, they ought gratefully to acknowledge their obligations to the Holy
Ghost, who condescends to perform his official work, in preparing them for the
kingdom of glory. . . .They are indebted to the person of the Holy Ghost, for all
love, repentance, faith, submission and every other Christian grace they have ever
exiercised. . .And it belongs to them who have received his gracious communica-
tions, to feel and express peculiar gratitude to him in particular.[53]

More than a few orthodox clergymen were to wish later that Emmons had
never printed this sermon on the trinity, for in the hands of their Unitarian
opponents it was a damaging piece. Emmons, of course, viewed himself as a
faithful trinitarian, but Unitarians viewed him as a virtual tritheist. The
oneness of the Godhead has disappeared behind a fog of mystery, while the
threeness of the distinctions in the Godhead operating in redemption and
the relation of man to each separately is the focus of interest. Emmons has
little difficulty discoursing upon ideas of the personality and agency of the
Godhead in time, but any clear and comprehensive idea of the unity underlying this in eternity is missing. There is little or no attempt to relate the *ad
intra* and the *ad extra*, the immanent and the economic trinity.

From this rather unorthodox perspective, Emmons easily rejects the
doctrine of the eternal generation of the Son. He finds no foundation in
Scripture or reason for the eternal generation of the Son or for the eternal
procession of the Spirit, and he dismisses both as "eternal nonsense." He
finds in the eternal generation of the Son a doctrine that weakens the
divinity of Christ and therefore lends support to Arianism. His concern is
first to show that the Sonship of Christ is grounded in the divine nature and
not in the divine will: if the second and third persons of the trinity are the
product of the Father's will, then their divinity is endangered, since the
Father might have willed not to beget the Son and in turn produce the
Spirit. Second, the idea of the eternal generation of the Son

sets the Son far below the Father, as a creature is below the Creator; and sets the
Holy Ghost as far below the Son as He is below the Father; or rather it makes the
Holy Ghost a creature of a creature! There are no ideas we can affix to the words beget, produce, proceed, but must involve them in infinite inequality between the three
sacred persons in the adorable Trinity. On this ground we feel constrained to reject
the eternal generation of the Son, and the eternal procession of the Spirit, as such
mysteries as cannot be distinguished from real absurdities, and as such doctrines as
strike at the foundation of the true doctrine of three equally divine persons in one
God.[54]

As we shall see, there were those among the orthodox who read this with
considerable discomfort, and it should be no surprise that the issue of the
Sonship of Christ should emerge as a topic of considerable debate in New
England theology. A shadow had been cast, a foreboding sense that the
answer to the question "Who is Christ?" was not forthcoming as clearly as

in the past. The partial darkness of an eclipse had begun to obscure the once readily visible glory of God.

Emmons's chief line of defense not only for the trinity but for Christianity as a whole is its reasonableness. Sensitive to charges that the trinity is an absurdity, Emmons struck back forcefully, asserting that we may be required to believe mysteries, but that God certainly does not require us to believe absurdities. There is nothing repugnant to sound reason in the doctrine of the trinity, for, after all, we cannot presume that God exists in the same manner as we and other created things exist. The mode of divine existence is necessarily mysterious, and, unlike an absurdity, a mystery is not a violation of reason. "Trinity in unity is agreeable to reason, improved and assisted by divine revelation. It is reasonable to think that the eternal God should exist in a mysterious, incomprehensible manner, and when he tells us so it is reasonable to believe his declaration concerning his own existence."[55] In many respects Emmons could outdo most of his contemporaries in extolling the "reasonableness of Christianity," convinced as he was that "it is the reasonableness of this revealed religion that has convinced ninety nine in one hundred."[56]

There were others, however, who could not make out this distinction between mystery and absurdity and viewed it as a distinction without a difference. To be sure, attacks against the trinity were aimed at its unreasonableness, and Emmons is constructing a line of defense against this charge. However, as we shall see, the main argument against the trinity was that it is an unscriptural doctrine lacking any support in the sacred text. In Nathanael Emmons the rationalistic side of the Puritan heritage comes to the foreground, and "principles of Truth" displace affections of the heart. There is mystery operative in the life of man in the light of God, but ultimately the dramatic encounter between the finite and the infinite may be rationally appropriated. It may be argued that Emmons lived and moved in a milieu in which theoretical truths were of intense emotional and deep practical interest. For those nurtured in Calvinistic thought, the connection of theological propositions and religious emotions was perhaps a living reality. For many others, however, spiritual starvation set in because religious truth seemed to lack living expression. This vacuum contributed to the decline of New England Calvinism and prepared in turn for the rise of alternative forms of religious experience and expression.

With respect to the doctrine of the trinity, no grand pattern of thought emerges neatly and clearly in Edwards and his successors. What we may rather draw are some tentative conclusions that may assist in the search for a better understanding of late eighteenth and early nineteenth century American religious life and thought. The movement in time away from Edwards among those who might qualify as his successors appears, in terms of the doctrine of the trinity, as a development in which the stress is increasingly upon the threeness of the Godhead in the covenant of redemption with a subsequent softening of interest in the immanent trinity. In Christology, the outcome of this development is a rejection of the doctrine of the eternal generation of the Son. In each instance, the trinity was vigorously upheld as essential to the Christian faith, but in no instance is it the subject of an extended separate treatise. The affective and relational qualities of the trinity which characterized Edwards's presentation of the doctrine were increasingly sacrificed to efforts designed to show that the trinity is not an irrational absurdity. The result was a reduction of the doctrine of the trinity to an item of orthodoxy and the loss of a lively sense of its role as a principle of theological thinking. Finally, a lack of historical perspective emerged, as Edwards's successors were either too dependent on him or, where they would not or could not follow him, as in the case of the trinity, they were left with too few resources from the wider stream of Christian thought upon which to draw. A sense of the history of Christian doctrine became increasingly narrowed to the confines of New England, with a resulting theological parochialism. The rise of Unitarianism then appears less as a surprise and more as the result of a natural outgrowth of strains of throught at work in New England Congregationalism which simply could not absorb the tradition we have been tracing. This held true no less for the doctrine of the trinity and Christology than for the doctrines of man, sin, and grace. What these alternative patterns of thought were must now become the focus of our attention.

2   The Trinity as the Eclipse of God
The Unitarian Controversy
I

The drift of the churches of eastern Massachusetts away from their orthodox roots is a complex doctrinal and ecclesiastical saga. Even prior to James Freeman's introduction, in 1785, of substantial revisions in *The Book of Common Prayer,* signaling strong liberal tendencies within Anglicanism, many congregational ministers in the Bay area were receptive to more "broad and catholik" forms of religious expression. Charles Chauncy's *Seasonable Thoughts* of 1745 were presented in opposition to revivalism and the whole pietistic emphasis upon a specific experience of conversion. Others, including Jonathan Mayhew, Thomas Barnard, and John Prince, emphasized the benevolence and fatherhood of God, the free agency of man, and the rational and non-credal character of Christianity.

Regarding the doctrine of the trinity, departures from traditional views were few in number, slow in emerging, and cautious in content. It is not our intention here to retrace the long, drawn-out "Unitarian Controversy." Rather, our interest is in identifying the role played by the doctrine of the trinity in liberal Christianity's search for theological expression, especially as it relates to the nature of Christ and to principles of interpretation of Scripture.

The appearance in 1756 of Thomas Emlyn's *An Humble Inquiry into the Scripture Account of Jesus Christ,* with a dedication "to the Reverend ministers of all denominations in New England" by "a Layman," may serve as a watershed in delineating the course of criticism directed at the doctrine of the trinity and in turn the divinity of Christ. It is well known that Edwards sought to hold the line against an Arminian softening of the doctrine of man. Now his followers would have to bring forward another, less well-developed, aspect of his thought, in order to confront another movement on the rise in New England, one that threatened both the doctrine of the trinity and the divinity of Christ. Arianism became an increasingly attractive alternative to many New England clergymen, and although there may be no necessary connection between Arminianism and Arianism, the liberal drift in anthropology was accompanied by a similar course in approaching the trinity and Christology.

The crux of Emlyn's argument was quite simple: Christ is subordinate and subject to, distinct and derived from, God. "God is all in all, and the Son Himself subject under Him. Can anything be more expressive of an inequality between God and Christ?"[1] Attributing equality between Christ and God does violence to the plain language of Scripture. There is, argued Emlyn, simply no need to ascribe divinity to Christ who, as a man, is given all that is necessary to execute His office. Only by subordinating Christ is the unity of God preserved against those who encroach upon it by elevating Christ to a position beyond what is warranted by Scripture.

This bold statement of Arian views elicited a number of responses, among them a tract by Aaron Burr entitled *The Supreme Deity of our Lord Jesus Christ Maintained*. The center of Burr's argument against Emlyn is that the biblical texts referring to subordination mean only Christ's human nature, not his divine person. The obvious and literal interpretation of Scripture, as opposed to Emlyn's forced and figurative usage, will reveal that divinity is properly ascribed to Christ. Christ's Sonship is such that in His human aspect He is the Son of Man, and in His divine person He is the Son of God. Contrary to Emlyn's understanding of Sonship, Burr argues that Christ is not Son by creation, adoption, or office, but His Sonship resides "in the very foundation of the Deity, where neither our senses, nor our reason extend." Appealing to what he assumes to be "a common notion of Trinitarians," Burr rehearses the doctrine of the trinity as the ground for his argument in favor of the divinity of Christ and his view of Christ's Sonship. As one of the three real and distinct persons of the Godhead, Christ partakes of the divine essence. Burr has to make, however, what later becomes a rather damaging admission: "it is not pretended, that the Scriptures anywhere tell us in express terms, or in just so many words and syllables that there are three persons in the Godhead, or One Divine Essence."[2] However, the "gist" of Scripture is in the direction of three real distinctions in the Godhead, each of whom partakes equally of all the divine attributes and perfections. The designation of these distinctions by the term "persons" is not an altogether happy one, but, call them what you will, the distinctions are real, and although the precise nature of the distinctions is above the grasp of reason, this is no argument against either the truth of these distinctions or the real divinity of Christ.

Among other divines who chose to write in response to Emlyn's tract was the Reverend Caleb Alexander, who penned an essay on *The Real Deity of Christ, to which are added Scriptures on Extracts from Mr. Emlyn's Humble Inquiry*. Detecting and fearing the spread of the influence of English Unitarians in America, Alexander sought to stave this off by amassing biblical evidence that "Christ is properly God." He attacks Emlyn's notion that the Sonship of Christ is derived and dependent, asserting rather that it is uncaused and unoriginated. Indeed, he is even fearful that "the Trinitarians, it is probable, in asserting the Son's eternal generation, have yielded too much to the Arians."[3] The doctrine of eternal generation implies that the divine nature was communicated to the second person of the trinity, and Alexander is convinced that this is not a proper understanding of the biblical teaching of Christ's Sonship.

Emlyn's *Humble Inquiry*, and the debate sparked by it, was in many ways the signal for the beginning of a controversy that was to ebb and flow for nearly a century in New England. The quiet growth of liberal sentiment among such figures as Charles Chauncy, Jonathan Mayhew, and Ebenezer Gay proceeded without placing the doctrine of the trinity out front. In fact, the doctrine suffered from a rather benign neglect among such divines, who occasionally expressed reservations about it but preferred quiet discourse to the threat of controversy. A notable exception was John Sherman, author of *One God in One Person Only and Jesus Christ a Being Distinct from God, Dependent upon Him for His Existence and His Various Powers.* Sherman argued boldly that "the commonly received doctrine is inconceivable by the human mind, not merely as to the mode, but as to the fact. . . . There is nothing within the compass of nature, experience, or observation which illustrates the doctrine, or by which it can be illustrated," and he concluded that the trinitarian scheme was "either rank tritheism or the very ultimatum of absurdity" and urged others to join him in "clearing away the rubbish of mystery and absurdity from the Christian system!"[4]

However, the exchange of views among more liberal clergymen was broadened in 1786, when correspondence was initiated between Thomas Belsham of England and a number of New England liberals. Belsham collected, edited, and published excerpts and commentaries on some of these letters in 1812 as a chapter on "American Unitarianism" in his *Memoirs of the Life of Rev. Theophilus Lindsey.* Three years later this chapter from the *Memoirs* was excerpted by Jedidiah Morse and published separately in Boston "for the benefit of Christian churches in this country, without note or alteration." The tract consists largely of letters from the Reverend James Freeman of King's Chapel, Boston, and William Wells, Esq. The letters report on the progress of Unitarianism in America under the leadership of Thomas Oxnard in Maine, Joseph Priestley in Pennsylvania, John Sherman in backwoods New York, and a number of liberal clergymen in "the environs of Boston." Special note is taken of the "liberal spirit" in the university at Cambridge, the work of Joseph Stevens Buckminster, and the contributions of *The Monthly Review and The General Repository* to the spread of enlightened religion. Belsham concludes:

> I could wish to see all who are truly Unitarians openly such, and to teach the doctrine of the simple indivisible Unity of God, as well as to practice the rites of Unitarian worship. But I would not presume to judge for another. There may possibly be reasons for caution which do not occur to me, and of which I am not competent to judge. The time must however come, perhaps it is near, when truth will no longer endure confinement, but will burst forth in all her glory. The dull hollow rumbling at the bottom of the sea, which is scarcely noticed by the inattentive traveller who is gliding carelessly over the solid plate of ice which encrusts the surface, is, to the wary and experienced observer, a sure presage of the speedy and sudden explosion of the

immense superincumbent mass, and of the restoration of the imprisoned waves to nature freedom, to the consternation and often to the utter destruction of those who refuse to listen to the friendly premonition.[5]

Belsham's *American Unitarianism* no sooner appeared than it was reviewed in the *Panoplist* by Jedidiah Morse, who, in 1805, had been stung by the appointment of the liberal Henry Ware, Sr., to the Hollis Professorship at Harvard, and who now championed the orthdox cause with renewed strength. "We regard the appearance of this pamphlet as one of the most important events, which have taken place for many years, in reference to the interests of religion in our country."[6] For Morse, the tract confirmed a suspicion he had harbored for some time—that the history of religion in New England for the last thirty years was a downward course "to the very borders of infidelity." This was the result of a secret yet systematic apostasy from "the faith of the Protestant churches," and the time was ripe to contend earnestly for the faith once delivered to the saints. Morse complained bitterly of "a settled and persevering determination to prostrate orthodoxy and to substitute Unitarianism in its place," and he declared himself ready for a round of good honest religious controversy to settle the issues.[7] He lamented the state of religious affairs at Harvard, "the pride and glory of our western world;" he chided the liberals for their "fulsome adulation" of each other, which he found nauseating; and he concluded that "the predominant religion of the liberal party is Unitarianism, in Mr. Belsham's sense of the word."[8] Accordingly, once the hand of the liberals had been forced, separation was the only course open to the orthodox.

II

Morse's Review, with its charges of "hypocritical concealment" and its call for separation, could not go unanswered. The response came in *A Letter to the Rev. Samuel C. Thacher, on the Aspersions Contained in a Late Number of the Panoplist, on the Ministry of Boston and Vicinity* by William E. Channing, minister of the Church of Christ on Federal Street, Boston. Channing was particularly stunned by Morse's charge that all Unitarians were of Belsham's stripe, and he sought first to define Unitarians as those who hold that "there is no distrinction in the divine nature" and then to clarify his Christology by asserting "that a majority of our brethern believe that Jesus Christ is more than a man, that he existed before the world, that he literally came from heaven to save our race, that he sustains other offices than those of a teacher and witness to the truth, that he still acts for our benefit and is intercessor with the Father."[9] As to the charge of secrecy, Channing finds this "uncharitable and disingenuous dealing," for he has labored publicly "to cherish the most exalted views of Jesus Christ which are consistent with the supremacy of the Father. . .and I have always abstained most scrupulously from every expression which could be construed into an acknowledgement of the Trinity. We preach precisely as if no such doctrine had ever been known."[10] Why? "Because if it do not mean that there are three Gods, (a construction which its advocates indignantly repel), we know not what it means; we have not thought that we should edify common hearers by attacking a doctrine althogether inconceivable and wholly beyond the grasp of our faculties."[11] Channing was prepared to adhere strictly to an *intimate relation* between the Father and the Son, but he would by no means admit to a *personal distinction* in the Godhead. This difference in language he identified as the crux of the debate between Trinitarians and Unitarians.

Finally, the call for separation was the harshest blow of all, because differences were over a doctrine that has divided the church for ages and perplexed the minds of learned and simple alike. Why, asks Channing, should exemplary Christians be shunned "because we cannot adopt the language of our brethren in relation to a doctrine which we cannot understand, and which is expressed in words not only unauthorized in Scripture, but as we believe, in words employed without meaning (unless they mean that there are three Gods) by those who insist upon them." [12] Channing concludes by urging restraint in religious debate, warning against the dangers of heresy-hunting and divisions in the church, and suggesting that the present affliction be interpreted as a trial of Providence that "will purify our character and extend our usefulness, making us better men and ministers."[13]

But the issue was not to rest, for Channing soon found himself caught in an exchange of letters with Rev. Samuel Worcester of Salem, a correspondence that dragged to nearly two hundred fifty pages. Worcester's first *Letter* to Channing is a rather detailed line by line vindication of Morse's *Review*, in which Worcester chides Channing for hasty and inaccurate reading, for undermining the essentials of Christianity, and for attributing all virtue to the liberals and all vice to the orthodox. He suggests to Channing that the differences between the two parties are greater than differences of language and "are certainly of a nature to demand the most serious and earnest attention."[14] Channing responded to this challenge calling the letter a "cruel disappointment" in its attitude toward Unitarian beliefs and character. He was concerned to establish a number of points, among them the fact that Unitarianism is a biblical faith, adhering strictly to the text, "because we stop where Scripture seems to us to stop, and because we have a very deep and sorrowful persuasion, that our religion has been exceedingly defaced and corrupted by the bold attempts of theologians to give minute explanations of its general truths, and to cramp it with the fetters of systematic precision."[15] Among such corruptions, of course, is the doctrine of the trinity, "a doctrine which bears the strongest marks of inconsistency with the fundamental truth of all religion, the unity of God, and which for ages has perplexed and distressed the mind of almost every reflecting Christian."[16] To denounce fellow Christians and exclude them from the community of faith because of their refusal to accept this "most obscure metaphysical doctrine" is more than Channing can bear. He re-iterates his conviction that the similarities are far greater than the differences between Trinitarians and Unitarians, and "in fact, as the word Trinity is sometimes used, we all believe it. It is time that this word was better defined. Christians ought not to be separated by a sound."[17]

Worcester was quick to respond, joining Channing on the crucial issues of the nature of Scripture and the doctrine of the trinity. Both men agreed that the overarching issue was whether fellowship should be continued between two parties whose approaches to Scripture and trinity were so different. Whereas Channing minimized the differences, Worcester did just the opposite, charging that "rational Christians" through a "torture of criticism" denied the plenary inspiration of Scripture and thereby forced the sacred text to yield views conformable to their rationalism. Similarly, their denial of the trinity as a violation of reason was said to be unconvinc-ing, for the trinity is "a mystery, which we pretend not to comprehend, and which we would not undertake to explain."[18] But this is not a trait peculiar to the trinity: the world, and religion especially, is full of mystery, and reason must recognize its limits. For example, reason cannot comprehend the two natures of Christ—that he is both God and man, equal to the Father in his divine nature, subordinate and inferior to the Father in his human nature. Those who have rejected the trinity as unreasonable do the same with the two natures of Christ, thereby arriving at an erroneous estimate of who Christ is. Channing, of course, was convinced that he knew who Christ was, quite apart from anything having to do with the doctrine of the trinity, and he made this clear in his *Second Letter* to Worcester.

Sensitive to the charge that Unitarians elevate reason above revelation in their rejection of the trinity, Channing repeats his earlier statement that the basis of the Unitarian objection to this doctrine is that it is unscriptural, and that in fact Unitarians are only being faithful to the sacred text in re-jecting a doctrine which is the fiction of theologians. Were the trinity a doctrine of revelation, then Unitarians would submit readily to it. As for the Sonship of Christ, Channing cites the works of Samuel Clark and asserts that since "Scriptures have not taught us the manner in which the Son derived his existence from the Father, it is presumptuous to affirm that the Son was created, or that here was a time when he did not exist."[19] This is a plague on the houses of both Arians and Athanasians, each of whose understandings of Sonship go beyond the light of Scripture to speak where silence should reign. The mode of Christ's derivation is left in obscurity by Scriptures, which, however, convey the impression that they "ascribe to Jesus the character of Son of God in a peculiarly high sense, and in a sense in which it is ascribed to no other being."[20] Finally, Channing continued to search for points of similarity rather than differences, convinced that the majority concurred on the great issues but differed primarily on the secondary issues of "first, whether One God be three distinct subsistences, or three persons, or three 'somewhats' called persons. . .and secondly whether one of these three subsistences of improperly called persons, formed a personal union with a human soul, so that the Infinite mind and a human mind, each possessing its own distinct consciousness, became a complex person."[21] When Trinitarians begin to explain themselves on these matters, "their three persons vanish into three *undefinable somethings,*" and "if they would tell us what they mean, their system would generally be found little else, than a mystical form of the Unitarian doctrine."[22]

Virtually every point in Channing's letter did little but try Worcester's patience in the extreme, and his *Third Letter* to Channing is a lengthy defense of orthodox views, beginning with the nature of Christ's Sonship. Sonship by no means denotes inferiority as Unitarians are fond of demonstrating, for if we assume the trinitarian distinction of persons in the Godhead, the charge that Christ cannot be at once the Son of God and himself also God is easily refuted. "If there are in the Godhead three Persons, Father, Son, and Holy Spirit, and each of these three in inseparable union with the other two is God; then there is no absurdity in saying that Jesus Christ is both the Son of God and himself God."[23] Channing, on the other hand, had left this issue so uncertain that the Sonship of Christ seemed a matter of "cold and lofty indifference."

Worcester next took it upon himself to lecture Channing roundly on "a plain and Scriptural exhibition of the doctrine of the trinity." The trinity is a plain matter of *fact* which is open to reason and can be understood. We can understand facts which are revealed; the element of mystery comes in what lies beyond, in what is not revealed, in the *how* of facts. That God is a trinity is a plain fact; how God is a trinity is a mystery. Worcester's primary argument for the trinity, however, is as follows:

> in the most Holy Three in One, we see what can never be seen in a single divine Person—we see a *society*, infinitely perfect and blessed. When we turn our thoughts from the Trinity to one Divine Person, who inhabits eternity in solitary existence, we find it impossible to conceive how he can be happy. We can form no conception of happiness without love, not perfect happiness where love has not an adequate object. . .The three adorable Persons, unlimited in all perfections and excellencies, inhabit eternity together; dwell everlastingly in each other, in mutual, perfect, unmeasurable love. Thus infinitely happy themselves, they unitedly delight in communicating happiness to their creatures. . .Call this, Sir, mystery, mysticism or what you please; it is a theme on which my mind delights to dwell; and which I cannot exchange for the solitary Deity, and the philosophical heavens of Unitarians.[24]

Doubtless by this point in Worcester's *Third Letter* Channing had stopped reading, and the exchange of letters broke off here, with a sense that the chasm between the two was unbridgeable.

III

Among those who became increasingly disenchanted with traditional statements of the trinity was Noah Worcester, sometimes cobbler, farmer, preacher, editor, and author of *Bible News, of the Father, Son and Holy Spirit*. The publication of *Bible News* resulted in Worcester's dismissal from his pulpit, but his disaffection with the Athanasian Creed could not be contained, and even though it meant a radical transition in his thinking, he adopted Arianism with enthusiasm. Worcester was convinced that the simple and natural, as opposed to the metaphorical and mystical, interpretation of Scripture will clearly show that Christ is not self-existent, but a derived and dependent being. Early in his treatise Worcester isolates the problem of language as the crux of the issue and proceeds to criticize the use of the term "persons" to describe the distinctions in the Godhead. The problem is, quite simply, what does the term mean when employed in this manner? "If I say that Father and Son are two distinct Persons, I ought to be willing to tell what I mean by the word Person."[25] While it is true that God is incomprehensible, still the language we use in discussing the nature of God is not incomprehensible but should have some meaning; to date, Trinitarians have simply failed to ascribe any meaning to the word "persons."

As to the usage of the term Son of God, it can, if properly understood, be truly applied to Christ. "For although there is perhaps, no one point in which Christians are more universally agreed than in calling Christ the Son of God, there is scarcely anything about which they are more divided than that of the intended import of those terms."[26] The orthodox have simply missed the meaning of this title, which is used in Scripture to denote Christ's derived and dependent character. However, to deny the self-existence of Christ is by no means to deny that He is truly the Son of God. True Sonship consists in derivation and suffering, in bearing the attributes of God but not the being or essence of God. The Son is not eternal, independent, and infinite, but in the plain language of Scripture and the simple faith of the primitive Christian community, the Son is sent as the begotten One subordinate to the Father. Noah Worcester is an especially interesting and important figure because of his clear change of opinion respecting the trinity and the divinity of Christ. He reports that he became embarrassed by the notion of "the covenant of redemption, in which mutual agreement was entered into by the Three self-existent and co-eternal Persons, respecting that part which each should perform in the work of redemption."[27] Citing Samuel Hopkins as a source of these obectionable views regarding the economy of redemption and the notion of a society of persons in the Godhead, Worcester laments: "I am grieved, that a man so eminent should do so much to expose Christianity to the ridicule of unbelievers."[28] Both the proper Sonship of Christ and the covenant of redemption are preserved and understood correctly only if the dependence of the Son and not His self-existence is made a pillar of the faith.

Anticipating the objections of his orthodox opponents, Worcester assures them that such a view of the Sonship of Christ does not lower His excellence and glory, but quite the reverse. For example, whereas formerly he could make no sense under the Athanasian scheme of the term "Person," now the term is alive for him, pointing to the distinct and exalted, yet derived and dependent, character of Christ. Worcester breaks off his espousal of Arianism by assuring his readers that he has no taste for controversy and no eye to personal gain and that "it is far from a pleasant thing to me to be obliged to dissent in opinion from such a multitude of worthy characters."[29]

Thomas Andros reviewed Worcester's *Bible News* in a *Letter* to "a friend inclined to credit that news," and warned that it was "not correct." Worcester had denied the eternal Sonship of Christ by asserting that, if He is "begotten," this term makes a "palpable contradiction" of eternal Sonship. Andros denied that a contradiction existed here, and he neatly escaped the dilemma by claiming that "at an unknown period in eternity the Son is begotten." As to Worcester's objection to the use of the term "person," it is a term "implied in Scripture" and therefore warranted in trinitarian usage. He chides Worcester for employing "his time and excellent talents to unhinge the faith of plain and upright Christians. . .who never were tempted by philosophical pride to imagine they could comprehend the doctrine of the Trinity; or that in order to their being Christians they must explain the ground of the property of terms being applied to God, which imply the existence of personal distinctions in the Divine Nature."[30] These were noble sentiments, if not very convincing arguments, in defense of orthodoxy.

Worcester also drew a response from Aaron Kinne, whose *Essay on the Sonship of Jesus Christ, with remarks on the Bible News by N. Worcester*, sought to clarify the point that the Sonship of Christ "does not immediately respect the Divinity of Christ." In fact, Sonship is an attribute separate from divinity and applies to the humanity of Christ. This distinction leads Kinne to reject the doctrine of eternal generation on the grounds that it has little support in Scripture and none in reason, "being inconsistent and repugnant to every dictate of common sense."[31] Sonship is a category that has its source in the incarnation and does not come into being until the conception in the womb of the Virgin Mary. Any notion of the Sonship of Christ antecedent to His appearance in the flesh is "too obscure to be comprehended and too absurd to be admitted."[32] Throughout his *Essay*, Kinne assures his readers that he has opted for the human Sonship of Christ in order to protect His true divinity and that his views are neither a distraction from the doctrine of the trinity nor a drift in the direction of Arianism. Exactly what the nature of the trinity is prior to the incarnation is left unclear. What is becoming evident is that confusion and controversy surround the Christological implications of the doctrine of the trinity in early nineteenth century American Protestant thought.

Worcester had extolled the simplicity of primitive Christian belief and urged the common sense and naturalness of this faith upon his readers. A similar argument is pursued by William Ware in a sermon on "The Antiquity and Revival of Unitarian Christianity," published in 1813. Ware adopted a perspective that was to prevail throughout much of the ensuing literature of the Unitarian controversy, that Unitarianism was the only religion of the New Testament. If read in its proper light, the New Testament, according to Ware, is "a history of the origin and early progress of Unitarian Christianity," which persisted through the third and fourth centuries until corrupted by Platonism.[33] The drift from Unitarianism to Athanasianism, from pruity to corruption, was the result of theological confusion and political intrigue in an age of barbarism and persecution. As a consequence, Unitarianism lay dormant until the Reformation, when its glorious revival was begun and the purgation of such corruptions as the trinity resumed. Ware's view of church history is subsequently governed by this interpretive principle of the decline and revival of Unitarianism, with the present age the culmination of truth's triumphal march.

In 1817, Thomas Worcester sought to put an end to the debates by publishing *A New Chain of Plain Argument Deemed Conclusive Against Trinitarianism*. This series of *Letters* rehearses all of the favorite Unitarian themes, including the lack of texts explicitly favoring the trinity, the absence of the trinity among the Jews of the Old Testament, who held to a firm confession of the unity of God, and the argument that the trinity was the product of fourth century wrangling and corruption. Further, the diversity of theories used to express the trinity is a traversty to the simplification of Chistianity, and the spirit of exclusivism exhibited by Trinitarians in all of their debates with those who disagree with them is a blot upon religious toleration and the spirit of the times. In short, "it appears to me impossible for any rational creature to remain a trinitarian after a patient, impartial, and thorough examination of the subject."[34]

IV

Perhaps this sampling of opinion will serve to demonstrate that the doctrine of the trinity came increasingly to the foreground as a topic of discussion, and open debate on it was no longer avoidable. That Unitarianism was spawned by other forces is undeniable, but the role of genuine confusion and controversy about the trinity and its Christological implications has too often been overshadowed by attention to other issues. The stage was set, then, for a major statement of the Unitarian position, which came in one of the most remarkable sermons in American letters, preached

at the ordination of Jared Sparks by the Reverend William Ellery
Channing.

The sermon, simply entitled "Unitarian Christianity," was delivered in
Baltimore on May 5, 1819, before an auspicious gathering of liberal clergy,
many of whom had made the trip from Boston especially for the occasion.[35]
The choice of Channing as standard bearer could not have been better, and
he delivered with eloquence a finely crafted party platform. A man of re-
fined taste and delicate sensibilities, Channing presented impeccable
credentials: a grandfather who was a signer of the Declaration of
Independence, a father who was a classmate of James Madison at Princeton
and later served as Secretary of State, a household that welcomed such
guests as George Washington. The influences of his youth included the
rather stern Presbyterianism of Princeton and the Puritanism of Ezra Stiles,
the Edwardean "new divinity" of Samuel Hopkins who was Channing's
pastor in his hometown of Newport, Rhode Island, and the liberalism of
Harvard College from which he was graduated. He was described as a
"serious, overthoughtful youth, inclined to self-inspection but acutely
sensitive to conditions of life around him."[36] He was ordained in 1803, the
same year in which he was called to the influential Federal Street Church in
Boston, where he remained until his death in 1842.

Channing outlined his program with consummate skill, beginning with
the principles of Scripture interpretation that will largely determine how the
doctrines of the trinity, the atonement, the two natures of Christ, and the
moral perfections of God will be presented. The foremost principle of interpretation is a consideration of the Bible as any other ancient writing, taking
into account its language, historical context, and the people to whom it is
addressed. "The Bible is a book written for men in the language of men,
and its meaning is to be sought in the same manner as that of other
books."[37] The search for meaning in the Bible requires the use of reason in
interpretation, for the language of the Bible does not have a fixed meaning
and therefore admits to various interpretations. The figurative language of
the Bible requires constant use of man's highest faculty, for reason is not at
war with revelation and those who disparage reason only give counsel to
darkness and error. "Revelation is addressed to us as rational beings," and
in His infinite wisdom God has adapted Himself to the capacities of man,
not to perplex and confuse him, but to enlighten and uplift him. Rational
principles of interpretation applied to Scripture will demonstrate that the
doctrine of the trinity is not a biblical teaching but a metaphysical construct. Once metaphysics is left behind in favor of biblical theology, the
repristination of Christianity will follow, and men will see clearly such
things as the unity and simplicity of God.

Putting these principles of interpretation into practice involves, then,
in the first place, "the doctrine of God's unity, or that there is one God, and
one only." A reading of Scripture reveals that God is "one being, one

mind, one person, one intelligent agent, and one only. . .," and the people to whom Scripture was addressed understood God as such.[38] Channing finds subversive the notion that the persons of the trinity have their own particular consciousnesses, wills, and perceptions, loving and conversing with each other in a society of persons, each of whom fulfills a different part in man's redemption. The effect of this teaching on the minds of simple believers is tritheism, and Channing is at a loss to know how the trinity can mean anything else. Further, he finds unconvincing those "hairbreadth distinctions between being and person which the sagacity of later ages has discovered" as an attempt to escape tritheism.

Channing admits that one person can be God, i.e., the Father, but nowhere in the New Testament does he find the faintest suggestion that the word God means three persons. Trinitarian claims about distinctions in the Godhead are simply misplaced, because if such a doctrine as the trinity were fundamental to Christianity, the New Testament would abound with evidence for it. Certainly, if this doctrine were a vital part of early Christianity, controversy would have surrounded it and the energy of the apostles would have been absorbed by attempts to repel assaults upon the teaching of three persons in one God. As it is, the evidence of Scripture overwhelmingly favors the unity of God, and the notion of trinity is an invention of language wholly unsanctioned by the Bible.

Channing's final objection to the doctrine of the trinity is drawn from practical considerations—it is "unfavorable to devotion." The mind of the worshipper is distracted and divided among three distinct persons, rendering communion with God impure: "Must not devotion be distracted by the equal and rival claims of three equal persons, and must not the worship of the conscientious, consistent Christian be disturbed by an apprehension lest he withhold from one or another of these his due proportion of homage!"[39] Further, because of human weakness which prefers an object of worship like ourselves, the trinity tends to accommodate this weakness by elevating the second person in Christian devotion. This unnecessary confusion makes the Son the most attractive person and relegates the Father to a secondary position of law-giver and judge. The essence of true piety is rather a deep awareness of the moral perfection of God, which the doctrine of God's unity enhances.

The Christological implications of adhering strictly to the unity of God and rejecting the trinity are explored next. The consequences of the trinity to Christology are "an enormous tax on human credulity," for "it makes Jesus Christ two beings, and thus introduces infinite confusion into our conception of his character."[40] Not content to make a triad of the Godhead, Trinitarians make a duality of Christ, ascribing to Him both divine and human characters, all without a shred of scriptural evidence. Again, just as with the doctrine of the trinity, had such a teaching as the two natures of Christ been such an important part of primitive Christianity, the

New Testament would abound with evidence for it. As it is, only a contortion of language and a departure from New Testament usage will produce the doctrine of the two natures of Christ. There is a unity to God and a unity to Christ, whereby the latter is not the one God, not the same as the Father, but distinct from and inferior to the one God. If there are a few texts that hint at the divine properties of the Son, the proper application of rational principles of interpretation will dispel these. The tone of Scripture is against the idea of the proper Godhead of Christ. "We say that it is one of the most established and obvious principles of criticism, that language is to be explained according to the known properties of the subject to which it is applied."[41] Divinity is not one of the known properties of Christ, as His birth, suffering, and death readily testify. In fact, ascribing divine Sonship to Christ "weakens our sympathy with His sufferings, and is, of all others, most unfavorable to a love of Christ, founded on a sense of his sacrifice for mankind."[42] That Christ truly suffered as a man is a view far more affecting on the heart than that view which ascribes both divinity and humanity to Him and then allows only the human nature to suffer. These difficulties are avoided by believing that there is one God and that Jesus Christ is a being distinct from and inferior to God.

These views on the trinity and Christology in Channing's Baltimore sermon are in many respects an elaboration of his correspondence with Worcester, and they are topics to which he returns throughout his career. The circulation of this sermon exceeded that of any publication prior to the Webster-Hayne debates of 1830, and Channing's influence in the spread of basically Arian views is important. Channing was interested in setting forth a clear, intelligible, and simple doctrine of God, which would be suited to apprehension by human reason. He was quick to read the signs of the times: the rise of biblical criticism, the growth of rationalism, the spread of republicanism. The spirit of the times simply outgrew the obscurities of such doctrines as the trinity, for the chief end of religion was, in Channing's view, to promote piety or reverence for God. The unscriptural and irrational teaching of the trinity hardly promoted this end, breeding rather a hybrid worship of three persons which, in fact, does not truly lift men to God. Thus, the notion "of one God, consisting of three persons or agents, is so strange a being, so unlike our minds. . .so misty, so incongruous, so contradictory . . .that to commune with such a being must be as hard as to converse with a man of three different countenances, speaking with three different tongues."[43] In place of the trinitarian formulation with its confusion of persons must be put a simple doctrine of the Infinite Father, which preserves both God's majestic glory and His paternal concerns. The doctrine of the trinity obscures the glory of God, which "is to do greater wrong than to blot out the sun," and it hinders a proper conception of the paternal nature of God.

3 The Trinity as the Distinctions of God

Moses Stuart and Samuel Miller

I

Channing's sermon on "Unitarian Christianity" attracted attention from a number of quarters, including Andover Seminary which had been founded in 1808 by a coalition of Old Calvinists and Hopkinsians in reaction to the liberal drift at Harvard. The so-called Andover Creed echoes their efforts to agree upon the seminary's theological basis, affirming among other things that "in the Godhead are three persons, the Father, the Son and the Holy Ghost; and that these three are one God, the same in substance, equal in power and glory. . . ."[1] Faculty members were obliged to reaffirm their adherence to this Creed every five years in what amounted to a tenure of orthodoxy. Among those who pledged their allegiance to the Creed was Moses Stuart (1780-1852), who in 1810 was summoned from the First Church of Christ Congregational in New Haven to the position of professor of sacred literature at Andover.[2] Stuart was a precocious youth who was able to read at age four, digested Edwards's *Freedom of the Will* at age twelve, graduated from Yale two years after his matriculation, and was a member of the bar at age twenty-two. However, during his undergraduate years at Yale, Stuart had been aroused to things of the spirit by the powerful chapel sermons of President Timothy Dwight, whose ominous deliveries awakened many Yale students to the threats of infidelity and Jeffersonianism. Thus his vocational change from the bar to the desk, where Stuart distinguished himself as an outstanding and powerful preacher.

Despite considerable disappointment and much reluctance among many members of his New Haven congregation, Stuart was relieved of his pastoral duties and assumed his post at Andover. Although appointed professor of sacred literature, he did not know the Hebrew alphabet, his knowledge of Greek was only slightly better, and he had to start from the beginning to teach himself German. Spurred by his own massive intellectual energies, within three years Stuart had mastered Hebrew to the point where he set the type for and published his own Hebrew grammar. His command of German enabled him to translate several important articles and made him the American scholar best acquainted with German biblical criticism. His overwhelming work load nearly always strained his health to the breaking point, and so expansive were his mental energies that he had to be restricted to four hours of study per day, during which time he insisted upon not being interrrupted for any reason whatsoever. His influence extended to nearly fifteen hundred students who, under his watchful eye, were brought to revere the sacred text. Described as a "tall, muscular and lean man, with a sharp and eager face and with rapid, nervous movements," the orthodox thought they had in the Andover professor a formidable spokesman to answer Channing's challenge.

Stuart addressed himself to the issue in his *Letters to the Rev. Wm. E. Channing, containing Remarks on his Sermon recently preached and published at Baltimore*, the tone of which was remarkably conciliatory. He assures Channing that in the matter of the principles of scriptural interpretation there is not as much difference between Unitarians and Trinitarians as Channing might think and that "to a great part of these principles I give my cheerful and cordial consent."[3] The principles of interpretation claimed by the Unitarians do not belong exclusively to that school, and the orthodox agree fully, for example, that "the language of the Bible is to be interpreted by the same laws, so far as philology is concerned, as that of any other book."[4] It may be that in the application of these principles to specific texts differences of opinion may arise, but the proper use of reason should settle any marked differences of interpretation. On this point Stuart may have been somewhat too sanguine, and he drew both the scorn of the liberal Andrews Norton at Harvard and the wrath of the Old Calvinist Samuel Miller at Princeton.

The conciliatory tone of the *Letters* continues as Stuart turns specifically to the doctrine of the trinity. The problem, according to Stuart, is in Channing's presentation of the Trinitarian position which he has failed to understand and therefore has misrepresented as Tritheism. This misrepresentation is the result again of a too-exclusive claim on Channing's part, i.e., that only Unitarians appropriate the unity of God. This claim is Trinitarian property, too, and if properly understood, the doctrine of the trinity is not at variance with it. Lamenting the efforts of some who have skirted the bounds of human knowledge and indulged in attempts to explain the inexplicable, Stuart seeks to set the arithmetic of the trinity straight:

> That God is one; numerically one, in essence and attributes; the infinitely perfect Spirit, the Creator and Preserver of all things, the Father, Son and Holy Ghost, has *numerically* the same essence, and the same perfections, so far as they are known to us. To particularize, the Son possesses not simply a similar or equal essence and perfections, but numerically the same as the Father, without division, and without multiplication. The Son (and also the Holy Spirit) does in some respect, truly and really and not merely nominally and logically differ from the Father.[5]

Was this sufficient answer to Channing's charge that all Trinitarianism is essentially tritheism? It was, argues Stuart, because the use of the term "persons" to designate the distinctions in the Godhead is not to be made in a literal sense. In discussions about the trinity, the problem of language is, Stuart has to admit, a real one, and the orthodox are as guilty as any of employing terms in an imprecise way to illustrate a very difficult subject.

Stuart laments the introduction of the term "persons" into Trinitarian thought, but he admits that it cannot be given up at this point and its usage must therefore be clarified. The point is to see that the term "persons" is not applied literally to the Godhead, and once this non-literal usage is clear the term may be used to designate distinctions in the Godhead without in any way impairing the unity of God. "We profess to use it merely to designate our belief of a real distinction in the Godhead; and *not* to describe independent, conscious beings, possessing *separate* and equal essences and perfections."[6] Literalism is the road to tritheism, but if Channing would only consistently apply his principles of interpretation to the term "persons," the whole controversy over the trinity would fall to the ground. The distinctions in the Godhead designated by the term "persons" are real and not mere attributes of God or the mere names of different modes in which God reveals Himself to man, or even the different relations He had with man through the several persons of the trinity. But the term does not designate three independent, conscious beings who possess separate and equal essences and perfections.

However, if pressed to describe further what these distinctions are, Stuart's answer is simple and unequivocal: "I do not know."[7] The distinctions of the Godhead designated by the term "persons" are simply a *fact* revealed by Scripture: "I receive the fact that it exists, simply because I believe that the Scriptures reveal the FACT."[8] Beyond this revealed fact lies metaphysics and confusion, into which Stuart will not plunge. For example, one such attempt to probe the distinctions of the Godhead is the doctrine of the eternal generation of the Son. Stuart has to admit that he cannot

> attach any definite meaning in the phrase eternal generation. I cannot attach any
> definite meaning which consists with a tolerable explanation of these words, with
> out virtually conceding Christ is *not God supreme*. . . . The generation of the Son
> in his divine nature, however mysterious or incomprehensible, imports at least a
> derivation in some sense or other.[9]

The fact of the distinctions in the Godhead and not the definition of them is the important thing, and Stuart is severely critical of the Nicene Fathers for their descriptions of things that are beyond the province of reason. The result of this speculation has been a doctrine that threatens the independence and self-existence of the second person by implying that Christ is derived and dependent. Further, it is well past the time when enlightened Trinitarians should divorce themselves from an ancient Platonic philosophy of emanation which modern men could no more adopt than the belief that the earth is flat. No matter how much we venerate the Fathers and their Creed, we can no longer be bound by their philosophy, and Stuart concludes that "the terminology of Nicaea I cannot subscribe to," for it implies a derivation and dependence of the Son; "the Nicene Creed is not, I must confess, sufficiently orthodox for me."[10]

Stuart sought to defend with rigor against Channing the notion of three distinctions in the Godhead and to defend with equal rigor against certain of the orthodox the absolute self-existence and independence of Christ. Against Channing, who said there were no distinctions in the Godhead, Stuart simply said, "prove it"; neither Scripture nor reason can show that distinctions in the Godhead are self-contradictory or impossible. On the other hand, the doctrine of eternal generation goes too far in its attempt to describe the distinctions and claims too much by way of understanding the persons of the Godhead. We should rather rest content with the fact of distinctions and leave definitions alone, for neither the unity nor the distinctions of the Godhead can be fully defined. Language is at best an instrument of approximation and not precision, and we should remain content with what has been revealed in Scripture. The search is for a language adequate to express ideas regarding a doctrine that has been much abused in the history of the church. Nothing is to be gained and no one is going to be convinced by epithets or by patristic name-dropping or by proofs that Calvin helped to burn Servetus, or by a confusion of personalities with issues.

The conciliatory tone of the opening paragraphs of his *Letters* had faded somewhat by the time Stuart neared the end some two hundred pages later. Sensing that nothing less than the very nature of Christianity itself was at stake in the controversy, Stuart charged: "I must regard the opinions which you have avowed in your sermon to be fundamentally subversive of what appears to me to be the peculiarities of the Christian system."[11] Stuart was correct in asserting that this was no trifling matter, and he continued to apply his vast learning to a search for a clarification of his views on the trinity.

II

Evidence of his continued study may be seen in Stuart's protracted reading of German authors, notably Friedrich Schleiermacher's *The Christian Faith*. The Andover professor was impressed with Schleiermacher's profound apology for the Christian faith, and his presentation of the doctrine of the trinity was particularly striking because it was arrived at quite apart from the influences of historic creeds and confessions. Schleiermacher insisted that in any statement of the trinity "the three persons of the Godhead must be placed on a perfect equality. This, although everywhere and at all times demanded, has not been done by any of the public formulas of the church."[12] With this observation Stuart could not agree more, and he agreed completely with Schleiermacher's rejection of the doctrine of eternal generation as a mode of expression which necessarily conveys a relation of dependence and inequality. While the pre-eminence of the Father over the Son was acceptable orthodoxy for both the Latin and the Greek fathers, it was not orthodox enough for either Schleiermacher or Stuart. In short, "the true method of representing the doctrine of the trinity has not yet been hit upon or achieved in the common Symbols." As Stuart read on, it seemed as though the late professor in the University of Berlin was describing the very tensions of New England itself: "the doctrine of the trinity still remains, according to the tenor of these symbols and the books of theology, in a state of oscillation between subordination and equality on the one hand, and on the other betwen Tritheism and such a Unitarian view as is inconsistent with the appropriate honours due to the Redeemer, or with the confident trust in the eternal efficacy of his redemption."[13] As he surveyed the field of battle. Stuart was quite sympathetic to Schleiermacher's call for a "new effort to make a more consistent and unexceptional representation of the doctrine of the trinity. . . ."

Schleiermacher closed the brief paragraph on the trinity at the end of *The Christian Faith* with a hint that in some forthcoming publication he would trace the causes of failure to represent the trinity in a more satisfactory form. The victory of the Nicene Creed as a reaction against Sabellianism, and an imprecise use of the term "Son of God" to designate the divine nature of the second person were suggested as issues worth further inquiry. When Schleiermacher did publish a separate essay on the trinity, Stuart took it upon himself to provide American readers with a translation of the essay in *The Biblical Repository and Quarterly Observer* under the title "On the Discrepancy Between the Sabellian and Athanasian Method of Representing the Doctrine of the Trinity." The essay is an important piece in the history of doctrine, as Schleiermacher seeks to correct misrepresentations of Sabellianism and to publish his sympathy with this view of the trinity.

Stuart appended his own extensive introduction and notes on the essay which make clear both his attraction to and his distance from Sabellius and Schleiermacher. Building upon his earlier *Letters* to Channing, Stuart resumes his attack on the Nicene Fathers and their theology of derivation and dependence of the second person, a method of viewing the trinity which no enlightened modern Trinitarian can accept. What is acceptable to moderns is a view of the trinity whereby the personality, but not the substance or essence of the second and third persons, is derived and dependent. In this way the doctrine of eternal generation can be jettisoned, the absolute equality of the persons in the Godhead protected, and the whole notion of the Sonship of Christ referred only to His mediatorial role.

The overriding issue is the question of the personality and what is meant by personal distinctions in the Godhead. Is personality, as used here, the product of time, of eternity, or of both? The Nicenes opted for the eternity of the dictinctions and developed the doctrine of eternal generation to protect their position. The Sabellians resolved the issue by asserting that the distinctions commence in time and develop only after the creation. Stuart was unhappy with both these representations of the trinity and was convinced that the truth was somewhere between the two extremes.

> There is a reason or ground in his very being for his developments as Trinity; else
> they would not be made. These developments necessarily pre-suppose some distinc-
> tions belonging to his nature. . . .we come by necessity then, at least so it seems to
> me, to the position that there was in the Godhead, antecedent to creation and re-
> demption, something which was the foundation of all the development of the same
> . . . .If you ask me how this modification or property or distinction can be described,
> as it originally existed in the Godhead, my answer is, that we have no data by which
> we can make out a description.[14]

There is something in the Godhead that allows for a development of personal distinctions in the economy of redemption, and the trinity is therefore
a revealed doctrine. As to the nature of the distinctions belonging to the
eternal essence of the Godhead, Stuart will not speculate, for this lies
beyond reason and revelation.

The distinctions in the Godhead are, then, in some way eternal, but it
literally takes time to develop them.

> The names themselves, Father, Son and Holy Ghost, are names not so much to
> characterize the original distinctions in the Godhead, as those by which the Godhead
> is disclosed to us in the scheme of redemption. . . .Distinctions in his nature God
> always possessed. But they were not developed before the scheme of redemption
> began.[15]

The incarnation does not initiate, but it does allow for, the full and
appropriate development of the trinity. Thus, the prior issue of the nature
of personality as applied to the Godhead is resolved by the assertion that "if
personality belong to the Godhead, it must belong to it, as it would seem,
not as *essential* to divinity, but as in some respect or other *modal*, or at least
as an attribute which holds (in a logical arrangement) a secondary and not a
primary place."[16] Stuart is willing to allow then that the Father begets the
personality of the Son but not his essence, and the Sonship of Christ desig-
nates not an eternal distinction in the Godhead but a development in time.

The trinity is, above all, a practical truth suited to "the needs of man as
sinner," and its soteriological importance must not be obscured by puzzling
speculations. Too long the orthodox have engaged in patristic squabbles,
metaphysical flights, and repulsive fits of language. The simple language of
the Bible must be restored in favor of the subtleties of controversy, and,
guided by reason and candor rather than love of creeds, metaphysics, and
tradition, men will be led to the simple truths of sacred writ.

III

Stuart's presentation of the orthodox cause did not meet with universal
approval from those whose position he made bold to represent. From the

chair of Ecclesiastical History and Church Government in the Theological Seminary at Princeton, Samuel Miller viewed the developments in New England with shock and dismay. Especially disturbing was Stuart's handling of the Nicene Creed and his rejection of the doctrine of eternal generation. In his *Letters on Unitarianism,* addressed to the members of the First Presbyterian Church of Baltimore, Miller stated: "the doctrine of the eternal generation of the Son is as closely connected with the doctrine of the Trinity and the Divine character of the Saviour, that where the former is generally abandoned, neither of the two latter will be long retained. . . .I therefore warn you against the error of rejecting this doctrine, even though it comes from *the house of a friend.*"[17]

Stuart was sufficiently impressed by Miller's sincerity and scholarship on the matter of eternal Sonship to make public his own extended research on the subject in his *Letters on the Eternal Generation of the Son of God, addressed to the Rev. Samuel Miller, D.D.* He begins by apologizing to Miller for not knowing "the doctrine of eternal generation was looked upon by Christians in our country to be so precious and important a truth. . . . During all my theological life I have never *once* heard the doctrine of eternal generation seriously avowed or defended."[18] Stuart informs his addressee that he did not intend to be rude or to offend his brethren at Princeton, for indeed this would be a most improvident time for a theological breach between New England and those to the South. He assures his orthodox colleague that rejection of the doctrine in question is not as impious and dangerous as he might think, and to be charged with views verging on Unitarianism was most injudicious. Certainly Christian charity permits those within the orthodox camp to have their differences without divisions. Together they should join in the established Protestant principle of subjecting all doctrines to the test of Scripture, on which ground Stuart is convinced that eternal generation was tried and found wanting. The progressive unfolding of Christian doctrine has allowed greater truth to burst upon the gospel since the days of the Fathers, and we of the present may no longer take refuge in the authority of their teaching.

Further, a critical examination of "the great body of early and influential Christian Fathers, whose works are extant, believed that the Son of God was begotten at a period not long before the creation of the world; or in other words that He became a separate 'hypostasis' at or near the time when the work of creation was performed."[19] Stuart's Christology subsequently revolves around a distinction of Logos and Son: "The Logos is eternal. . .but that the Logos was eternally the Son of God, I doubt. . . ."[20] The problem is that Miller and others have confused the terms creation and generation as applied to Son, a confusion the Fathers did not make because to them the terms meant the same thing. The Fathers were guilty, however, of falling victim to the philosophy of the time and of applying it to the manner in which the distinctions or persons of the Godhead are related to each other. The result was a corruption of the simplicity of Scripture and a violation of reason. But Stuart rejoices: "I cannot but feel gratitude to God that he has ordered my existence in an age when more Scriptural and rational views of his perfection are entertained. . . ."[21] The rarified atmosphere of German critical scholarship was heady wine for early nineteenth century America, and with it Stuart was prepared to brush aside the crude speculations of the Fathers to make way for more enlightened views. The movement from patristics to exegesis would accomplish this objective, and he admitted frankly that if the question "is to be decided by patristical or ecclesiastical authority, or by the voice of the majority of times past, I acknowledge you will have an advantage over me."[22] It is noteworthy that Stuart chose the doctrine of eternal generation as the one against which he would unleash the full force of his exegetical skills.

Stuart continued his attack by explaining the relationship betwen language and intelligibility. What is unintelligible or surpasses our comprehension belongs to things and not to words. What we express respecting things must be intelligible, and although there is mystery connected to both things and language, we cannot hide behind the veil of mystery when statements are made that are perfectly contradictory. The phrase eternal generation is "a palpable contradiction" which no juggling of language can make intelligible. Self-existence and derivation are mutually exclusive attributes which cannot be brought together in the phrase eternal generation, and the verdict of reason is that this is an "unmeaning and unintelligible " phrase that is incompatible with true divinity. The only way to resolve the problem is to understand that the Logos is self-existent and underived, while the Son is derived and dependent.

It belongs, however, not to reason but finally to Scripture to determine the meaning of Sonship. First, it is a mistake to place too much weight upon the title Son, since there is a wide latitude of meaning applied to it in Scripture, and especially in the Old Testament, there is a "very vague, indefinite and extensive" usage of the term. Second, it is a mistake of the liberals to assign Sonship to Christ on the ground of His moral resemblance to the Father. The Scripture is clear beyond question that Sonship applies to the human nature of Christ, "because, in respect to His *human* nature, He is derived from God."[23] The eternal Logos, then, cannot be designated as the Son, for it is the incarnation which properly gives rise to the title Son. "If the divine Logos was derived from the Father, was begotten from eternity and was therefore Son, in the highest sense, before the birth of Jesus, I am not able to understand how this birth could be the reason, why Christ should be called the Son of God."[24] The evidence of the Gospel of John, especially, is that not a word is uttered of the Son before the incarnation; pre-existence belongs only to the Logos.

Christ is also called Son of God by virtue of "the elevated dignity that was conferred on Him as Messiah."[25] It is the resurrection which elevates

Christ to this dignity, and after detailed examiniation of several texts, Stuart concludes that the *usus loquendi* of the term "Christ" among Jews and early Christians meant essentially the Son of God in this messianic sense. Nowhere in the Old or the New Testaments does the title Son carry the connotation that he was eternally and necessarily begotten of God. "If I am correct then, the Logos before His incarnation was not strictly speaking, Son of God, but only to become so by union with the person of Jesus."[26] If the term Son cannot be properly applied until the incarnation, the same must be true of the title Father. What then becomes of the immanent trinity? It seems for the moment to have disappeared behind "distinctions" in the Godhead which Stuart affirms but admits he could not explain. He is not at all sure

> that the terms Father and Son are used as a characteristic designation of original relations in the Godhead. . . .If the Father Son and Holy Spirit are words which designate the distinctions of the Godhead as manifested to us in the economy of redemption (which after the preceding investigation I cannot doubt) are not intended to mark the eternal relations of the Godhead, as they are in themselves, and in respect to each other; then we may easily account for these designations, without being obliged at all to recur to the supposition, which you [Miller] seem to think inevitable.[27]

The supposition was, of course, that when the doctrine of the eternal generation of the Son is given up, the doctrine of the trinity falls into decay, and with it the divinity of Christ. Stuart did not appreciate having his orthodoxy impugned, and he moved to demonstrate that his orthodoxy was more valid that that of the Old Calvinists of Princeton.

Again, it is the tension of the immanent and the economic trinity, of the internal distinctions in the Godhead and the manner in which they are revealed to man, that is at stake in the controversy. When Stuart exclaims almost in desperation "What *is* Christ?" he has arrived at the heart of the issue of the Christological implications of the doctrine of the trinity in the period between Jonathan Edwards and Horace Bushnell. This was the key question, provoked by the nature of Christ's Sonship and spurred on both by attempts to discredit and to restate the doctrine of the trinity. Perhaps historians have assumed too easily that the doctrine of the trinity suffered near total neglect in favor of disagreements over the nature of man and the doctrine of grace; this was not the case.

Stuart closed his *Letters* to Miller by reassuring the Princeton historian that his observations concerning the New England clergy were off the mark.

> The second generation of ministers is now passing from the stage in New England, who have rejected this doctrine; and apostacy has been no more frequent among them, than among the brethren who have embraced it. It is indeed true, that the stronghold of Unitarianism in this country is in the heart of New England. . . .But it remains to be shown, that the rejection of the doctrine of eternal generation was

the leading introductory step to our Unitarianism. Far different causes have oper-
ated in producing this effect. . . .[28]

Stuart tries to convince Miller that a united front among those of orthdox
sentiments is a desirable objective and that doctrinal differences should not
be inflated to party disputes.

Stuart was a formidable figure who contributed significantly to the rise
of biblical criticism in Ameria and who wrestled with the doctrine of the
trinity persistenly and vigorously. It is somewhat unfair to suggest that "his
minimal formulation of the trinity caused it to lose its place as the fundamental doctrine of the system."[29] He sensed the need for a restatement of
the doctrine and made some tentative movements in that direction. The task
of constructing the trinity upon a purely scriptural basis apart from creeds
and historic doctrine remained unfinished, if indeed it is a task that can be
accomplished at all.

                                    IV

Although his work load was staggering and the demands upon his time
were pressing, Samuel Miller (1769-1850) deemed the discussion with Stuart
important enough to take time for an extended response. Miller's every
word and action breathed orthodoxy of the Old Calvinist stripe, a heritage
he traced back to his sugar-refining, whiskey-distilling, Scottish Presbyterian grandfather. Miller was awarded a baccalaureate degree by the
University of Pennsylvania, and by age thirty he had held the two most
influential pulpits in Philadelphia and New York City. He was a natural
candidate when, in 1812, the trustees of the new seminary at Princeton went
searching for a professor of church history. Miller accepted the challenge of
this post which he assumed in 1813, and for thirty-six years he lent his extra-
ordinary energy and urbane manner to the cause of consistent Calvinism at
Princeton. In addition to his teaching responsibilities, Miller was a frequent
participant in denominational affairs, carried on a voluminous correspondence, was noted for his prolonged pastoral calls, and was contributor to
numerous periodicals as well as author of several books. The most famous
of his publications, A History of the Eighteenth Century, earned him
notoriety among intellectuals because of the breadth of learning displayed
in its account of the progress of both the sciences and humanities. Princeton
possessed in Samuel Miller the very Nestor of orthodoxy.[30]

Miller was alarmed by Stuart's concessions to the liberals, and his
own Letters on Unitarianism Addressed to Members of the First Presbyterian Church in Baltimore made clear that he considered Unitarianism as
infidelity, as "a system of error which I have no hesitation in considering as
the most delusive and dangerous of all that have ever assumed the Christian
name."[31] What is this party with whom there is to be no coming to terms?

Quite simply, they are "those who reject the Bible doctrine of *Trinity* in *Unity;* who contend that there is in Jehovah but one Person, as well as one essence; and who with the doctrine of the trinity, reject all the other *peculiar* and *fundamental* doctrines of the gospel."[32] They have come up "like the plagues of Egypt," and now is the time for the orthodox to engage in a warfare waged for all that is glorious in the Gospel." After this opening volley, Miller turns to a point-by-point defense of the trinity, beginning with the Unitarian charge that Trinitarians inevitably end up in a veil of mystery in dicsussing this doctrine. Miller responds by saying that mystery is the very stuff of the life of God and the life of man, and no amount of enlightenment thought can dispel it. The trinity is a superb example of the mysteriousness of existence. We are "utterly unable to comprehend it. We do not suppose that any man on earth ever did or ever can understand this august mystery."[33] As to the charge that Trinitarianism inevitably ends in tritheism, Miller responded that no right-thinking orthodox Trinitarian has ever denied the unity of God; this unity is as essential to the Trinitarian as to the Unitarians cause. But, "before any one undertakes to decide that a Trinity of Persons in God is inconsistent with the Divine Unity, he ought to be able to tell us what Unity is."[34] If Unitarians cannot define unity as ascribed to God. "we surely cannot be prepared to decide how far a Trinity of Persons in the Divine Essence is inconsistent with it, and involves anything like an absurdity or contradiction."[35] Further, no Trinitarian in full possession of his senses ever said that God is one in the same way that He is three. Again, it is not to be explained but received as a fact of mystery that God is one in one sense and three in another sense; to this more than a few Unitarians would simply respond that it makes no sense.

Another troublesome issue centered, as we have seen, around the use of the term "persons," and Miller joins the chorus of those who admitted that the poverty of language forces the usage of this term to express distinctions in the Godhead. The term cannot be dismissed, however, for the certain "threefold mode of existence" expressed by it is essential to the trinity. However, Miller made it clear that

> we utterly deny that we mean by it three distinct independent beings; for we believe that there is but one God. But we mean to express by it a certain (to us mysterious) threefold mode of existence, in the one living and true God, which carries with it the idea of an ineffably glorious society in the Godhead, and lays a foundation for the use of the personal pronouns I, Thou, He in that ever-blessed society."[36]

Was this sufficient answer to tritheists and Unitarians alike? To Miller's mind it certainly was, and everything is neatly put together with no problems left unsolved. On the one hand, Miller asserts that the doctrine of the trinity is an utter mystery. On the other hand, he promptly proceeds to explain it in terms of "the Bible doctrine of Trinity in Unity." He rejects the idea of "three distinct independent beings" in the Godhead, and yet he says that the Godhead embraces an "ineffably glorious society," a society about which one may properly speak of the members of the Trinity in terms of personal pronouns, "I, Thou, He." This inconsistency would appear to threaten the unity of the Godhead which Miller sought to protect. He is convinced, however, as Stuart was not, that the nicene Creed is grounded in the Bible and not Greek metaphysics, and he rehearses at length the testimony of the fathers as authoritative evidence for the essential agreement of Scripture and creed. He is irked by Stuart's attitude toward the fathers and the Nicene Creed, and he defends both as indispensable to the life and thought of the church. Creeds are especially important as a defense of the faith once delivered to the saints and as a bulwark against the threats of Unitarians and German theologians, and this certainly was not time for the orthodox to hang their harps on a willow and sit by the waters of Babylon while all around them heresy ran wild. Those who deny the trinity ought not to be granted Christian communion, and if the Congregationalists of New England were not prepared to enforce the Creeds of the church, the Presbyterians of Princeton were.

Some of Miller's strongest language, however, is reserved for his attack upon Unitarian principles of scriptural interpretation. He found their constant appeal to Scripture a "mere illusion," and their interpretation of it "one of the most conclusive evidences of the vital rottenness of their system."[37] Unitarians have elevated reason over revelation, and although the orthodox do not deny the role of reason in revelation, certainly reason alone is an insufficient guide to spiritual things. Unitarians, on the other hand, apply reason to the alleged facts and doctrines of revelation to determine whether these are reasonable, concluding *a priori* that such a doctrine as the trinity is unreasonable to man and unworthy of God. While the Bible may reveal doctrines that are above our slim portion of reason, Scripture does not reveal doctrines that are contrary to reason. The misuse of reason turns reading the Bible into a cold intellectual exercise and fractures the plenary inspiration of holy writ. The simplest peasant armed only with common sense can read the Scripture and arrive at the plain teaching of the trinity without the aid of Priestley, Belsham, and German theologians. New Englanders are free to flirt with biblical criticism if they wish, but Princeton will remain a seat of orthodoxy and common sense. In the words of one commentator, Miller was defending "an orthodox world that New England had not denied, but had with even more decisive effect merely forgotten."[38]

V

Samuel Miller was an historian of doctrine for whom "doctrine must be viewed in the light of personal experience, and not just nominally subscribed to; it is not a matter of speculation only."[39] It was a particular affront, then, when Moses Stuart summarily dismissed the doctrine of eternal generation because it made no sense to him. When Stuart published his *Letters* on the subject, Miller read them with care and responded with his own *Letters on the Eternal Sonship of Christ Addressed to the Rev. Professor Stuart of Andover.* "Letters" were a common medium of polemics and a gentlemanly way of carrying on a theological discussion while at the same time reaching a wider audience. Miller opens his *Letters* with a perfunctory acknowledgement of his dialogue partner for conducting the exchange on such a high level. With this polemical nicety discharged, however, he states bluntly: "Your arguments have totally failed of convincing me that the positions which I laid down are untenable."[40] As to the matter of eternal Sonship, the orthodox of Princeton consider it a "highly important" doctrine, and despite what the "orthodox" brethren of the North may say, the Presbyterians of the Middle Colonies by no means consider it a matter of small importance. Following his reading of Stuart's *Letters* to Channing, Miller writes: "I must confess that my pleasure in perusing them suffered considerable deduction on account of several things which they contained."[41] Among these "several things" was a denial of the eternal generation of the Son, and Stuart had placed in the hands of the Unitarians weapons that would surely be used against him. Stuart had compounded his error by publishing his *Letters* on eternal Sonship.

Miller summons Stuart to examine the history of New England theology and to acknowledge his departure from the faith of the fathers. A brief examination of the theology of Edwards, Bellamy, and Hopkins would reveal that they held strongly to the doctrine of eternal Sonship. The notable exception to this lineage was "the acute and venerable Dr. Emmons," but Miller has serious reservations about Emmons's stature as a theologian. While noting that he is not in a position to assess the current status of New England theology as a whole, Miller is convinced that beginning with Emmons many of the clergy of New England had wandered not only from the standard doctrine of the historic church but from their own historic standards. This rage for novelty and ardent love of originality he interpreted as "an unhappy symptom."

As we have noted, Stuart's main objection to standard presentations of the trinity was that they perpetuate a subordination of the second person. Not so, replied Miller, for the idea of a derived and dependent God was just as abhorrent to him, and he, too, objected to any notion of a personal and eternal subordination of the Son. Indeed, the doctrine of eternal Sonship was promulgated by the early Fathers to combat precisely that which Stuart said it promoted, i.e., subordinationism. Here the argument reached an impasse, and there is little evidence that either man moved the other to even a slight change in position. Disturbed by Sabellian tendencies in Stuart's position, Miller sought to convince him that Christ is Son not by a voluntary act of God's will but as a necessary attribute of God's being. The question is whether the titles Father and Son properly express an "official character" assumed in time or the necessary and eternal relations of the first two persons of the trinity? Miller made his position clear: the Father is Father *as such*, and the Son is Son as such, "not by incarnation, adoption, or office, but by *nature*. . . ."[42] There was, then, no necessary implication of subordination in the notion of eternal generation; in fact, just the opposite was the case—where the eternal Sonship is denied, the divinity of Christ is jeopardized.

Miller was now ready to confront Stuart on the critical issue of hermeneutics, hurling the challenge that "wherein the spirit of it differs from the principles of interpretation avowed and acted upon by our Unitarian neighbors, I acknowledge my utter inability to perceive."[43] Eternal Sonship is, of course, in Miller's view, a biblical doctrine, and only perverted principles of interpretation could lead to any other finding. How else are we to know God, for certainly the validity of revelation evaporates if the titles Father and Son commence only in time. What evidence would we have that God had not held something back, that He is not something else *ad intra* than He is *ad extra?* Is the trinity to be applied only to God in His revelation and not to God in Himself? A denial of eternal Sonship calls into question the reality and ultimacy of revelation as well as the inspiration of Scripture as a source of revelation. Miller was almost frantic as he detected the very essence of Christianity slipping away, and through the fingers of an orthodox colleague.

Further, Scripture teaches that without the eternal distinctions of persons in the Godhead whereby each has some peculiar relation to the others, an incredible confusion results. The trinity is a who's who of the Godhead, and to deny the eternal Sonship of the second person is to leave the first person without a title. These are titles that each person has in eternity, titles made manifest in time and the economy of redemption. "I have always supposed that the principle object of the economy of redemption was to glorify the triune God, by manifesting the appropriate or eternal distinctions of the Godhead; by shewing forth the true glory of God, as He is in Himself, more illustriously than it ever was or can be exhibited in any other way."[44] The doctrine of the trinity, then, expresses the paradox of God in Himself and God in relation. This tension and the paradox lies at the heart of the doctrine of the trinity. To stress the economic trinity at the expense of the immanent trinity does less than justice to God "as He is in Himself." To stress the immanent trinity at the expense of the economic trinity jeopardizes God in relation through the covenant of redemption.

Stuart's corrupted principles of interpretation, according to Miller, have also led him to misunderstand the term Son, which is not some "official character" bestowed upon the second person of the trinity by virtue of incarnation or resurrection. Sonship is a title of divinity and does not designate primarily the humanity of Christ. Stuart's distinction of

Logos as a designation of divinity and Son as a designation of humanity is an artificial construct that does violence to Scripture and gives aid and comfort to the Unitarians, who would like nothing better than to think that Christ was Son of God as a mere man. The denial of eternal Sonship threatens not only the doctrine of the trinity, but the unity of the two natures of Christ because it implies that there are two Sonships, one in time and one in eternity. Stuart's sterile and wooden *Logos* Christology was particularly upsetting to Miller, who found in it none of the eternal, paternal relationship of Father and Son. Even Unitarian representations of the relation of Father and Son are not so lacking in feelings! Again, the Christological implications of the doctrine of the trinity opened a breach within orthodoxy that was not soon to be healed.

As we have noted, Stuart affirmed repeatedly "distinctions" in the Godhead, but he admitted he could not explain them. He spoke almost not at all of relations in the Godhead, and, indeed, he found the idea of a society and covenanting transactions and deliberative counsel in the Godhead to be "particularly repulsive." Miller traced this consequence to Stuart's denial of eternal Sonship, for this

> leaves us without any titles of language which seem adapted to express close and endearing *relation* between the Persons of the ever blessed trinity. . .here would seem to be *no relation at all* between the Persons of the Trinity; that is, there seem to be no titles or representations, on your plan, which indicate related states between these Persons. . .In short, you seem to me to exhibit and to leave the subject, as to this point, under an aspect altogether unfriendly to Scriptural views of related Persons in one Triune Jehovah; and calculated to favor either Sabellianism on the one hand, or Tritheism on the other.[45]

The truth is that the persons of the Godhead are both united by ineffable relations and distinguished by incommunicable properties. It would appear that Miller is writing himself into the conviction that the trinity is less of a mystery than he imagined.

The real thunder of his argument is reserved, however, for an exhibition of patristic thought on the subject, a field in which he was most at home and through which he moved with skill and ease. In a lengthy report of the testimony of the early fathers on the eternal Sonship of Christ, Miller finds overwhelming evidence in favor of this doctrine. According to the testimony of the Fathers, the Son does not emerge in time to engage in creation and redemption; rather, the Godhead exists essentially and eternally as triune. To suggest, as Stuart did, that the *Logos* was formed into the Son just prior to the creation is an untenable proposal that warps the witness of the fathers into a kind of "patristic Unitarianism." Even though the language of the ante-Nicene Fathers was not perfect in every respect, they do not deserve the roughshod treatment that Stuart had accorded them.

The doctrine of the trinity not only raised the question of the authority, inspiration, and criticism of Scripture, it also precipitated a crisis over the authority of history and tradition. The authority of the church fathers and the role of patristical evidence in doctrinal disputes came under increasingly heavy attack. The weight of the past was a burden for some, such as Stuart, who willfully cast aside the baggage of patristics. There were others, such as Miller, for whom the search for a usable past was intensified by careful study in the history of doctrine and who found in the early fathers a source of authority and a link with the past that they refused to jettison. There were in turn those, such as Channing, who viewed the trinity as an unessential corruption of the faith, a product of tradition and speculation that could be laid aside with no threat. To the other side, there were those, such as Worcester, who viewed the trinity as a fundamental doctrine of Christianity from which all else derived and the loss of which would surely mean the end of the historic faith. There were those, like William Ware, who saw the rejection of the trinity as a road to the recovery of a primitive Christianity, while others viewed the same as the inevitable destruction of the faith once delivered to the saints. There were those who saw in the trinity a fundamental belief around which to order their thinking about the Christian faith, while at the same time there were others who saw in the rejection of the trinity a freedom to reflect more clearly upon Christianity and to practice it more faithfully. The doctrine of the trinity presented a crisis of beliefs and values that divided more than Unitarians and Trinitarians. It sent shock waves through the citadels of orthodoxy itself, arousing suspicion and dissension from sources least expected.

Miller closed his *Letters* with the hint that Stuart would do himself and the cause of orthodoxy a favor if he read more widely in the history of doctrine. Improper views of Christ's Sonship have always served as a wedge for Arianism, which in turn gives rise to Unitarianism. Miller was aware that the rise of Unitarianism in New England was not due exclusively to the demise of the doctrine of eternal generation, "but that it is *one and by no means the least*, of the real causes, cannot possibly be doubted, when I attend to the history of theological sentiment in that section of our country."[46] In the style of a good polemicist, Miller expresses the desire that his pen would not be active in this matter again. There is some evidence that his *Letters* forced Stuart into a wider reading of Christian doctrine; there is little evidence that they forced Stuart into any real change in his position.

VI

Samuel Miller was not the only one to monitor Stuart's defense of orthodox sentiments. "An Old Soldier of the Arian War" offered his strictures in *A Treatise Upon the Eternal Generation of the Son,* and defended the doctrine as "the first in order, and which lies as the foundation of all others. . . ."[47] The author tied the issue of personality in the Godhead to the doctrine of eternal generation, and he argued that

> they who deny the doctrine of eternal generation have no claim to the name of Trinitarians; for they also give up personality as belonging to the Trinity. This is of course; for if the Son was not begotten from eternity, the paternal and filial character and relations of Father and Son have not existed from eternity; and if the Father, Son and Holy Ghost have not existed from eternity, we have no evidence that three persons have so existed.[48]

The conclusion to the argument is somewhat strained, but the conviction of its author is real—that the doctrine of the trinity and the eternal generation of the Son are doctrines that express relations. Either to reject them or to reduce them to logic-chopping destroys the relational realities they were designed to express. The consequences of this omission for church life in New England was real and immediate:

> I can witness the facts, that the apostacy in Massachusetts Bay, commenced with giving up the doctrine of eternal generation, and that it was followed with a quick step, by the renunciation of the Trinity. The men who began the work, did not mean that it should be so consummated; but the generation succeeding them became Unitarians for two reasons, viz., they were never taught the true and only defensible doctrine of the Trinity; and they had too much sense to use terms, the meaning of which they did not understand.[49]

The "old soldier" was roused to arms by Stuart's *Letters* to Channing, and he accused the Andover sage of "believing no more than his brother in Boston, that the doctrine of the trinity can be defended." With his eyes cast to the Bay City, he laments, "O Boston! Where is thy golden candlestick, once shining with stars of angelic brightness!" First the holy city had succumbed to Unitariansim, or slid and fell on what he calls "the Boston glacier," and now Andover was about to fall, for Stuart was "essentially a Unitarian." "Is the man, whose mind is so confused upon this subject that he cannot write sense, qualified to pass sentence of condemnation upon the Nicene Creed?" This ancient symbol is so clear in its formulations that "even a Professor of sacred literature can understand it."[50] Again, intramural differences found the house of orthodoxy in such disarray that a united defense of the trinity was impossible.

Meanwhile, Miller's *Letters* drew the wrath of Jared Sparks, who as editor of the *Unitarian Miscellany* felt compelled to defend his party against Miller's unconscionable charges. A series of letters written for the *Miscellany* by Sparks was reprinted under the title of *An Inquiry into the Comparative Moral Tendency of Trinitarian and Unitarian Doctrines.* After a defense of the character and Christian charity of Unitarians, which Miller had impugned, Sparks turns directly to a discussion of the trinity. He reports having searched for a clear and concise statement of the trinity, but, alas, "theories of the trintiy have become as numerous as the writers by whom it has been attempted to be explained."[51] His survey of the literature convinced him that good men were driven to Unitarianism simply by "phrases of unmeaning import," and "the more the defenders of this doctrine say about it, the less intelligible they become, and the farther they receed from principles of common sense."[52] From this "chaos of incertitude" Unitarianism offers a sensible escape.

Sparks is especially incensed by Miller's assertion that the rejection of the trinity meant *ipso facto* the rejection of Christianity. He is at a loss to understand how the denial of a mysterious metaphysical notion could be construed as the denial of Christianity. He chides Miller for the phrase "mysterious threefold mode of existence" as a combination of words without meaning, as "mere sounds." The real force of his argument, though, is reserved for the denial of the trinity as a scriptural teaching. Surely it would have been a novel notion to the primitive Christian community that the trinity was a plain teaching of Scripture. We are not in a position to improve upon or to reject the faith of the early community, which clearly knew nothing of the trinity. It is, rather, a doctrine arrived at by "inference," without direct evidence from Scripture, and to make the trinity a standard of faith is a plain violation of both the sacred text and of religious liberty.

As to the "moral tendency" of Unitarian doctrines, Miller's fears of apostasy and the corruption of society were simply unfounded. In fact, much more is to be feared from the moral tendency of Trinitarianism, for this system destroys the simplicity of Christian worship by distracting the believer and distributing his affections among three "persons." Clearly, to Miller, "the evil consequences of this doctrine, if they are not checked by others more rational in their nature, and practical in their tendency, would overthrow the whole system of revelaion and leave nothing but a heartless infidelity."[53] The doctrine of the trinity was presented by its defenders as essential to the stability and well-being of the social order, while its detractors argued precisely the opposite. Right doctrine was important not only to the explication of the faith, but for the wider implications of society.[54] Each side argued that the "moral tendency" of the other's view issued in infidelity and a weakened social fabric. For all concerned, doctrine was not an incidental matter debated by arm-chair theologians, but a vital part of the milieu in which they lived and worked. Like the doctrines of original sin and the atonement, the doctrine of the trinity got caught up in the argument from "moral tendency," which in the end may be no argument at all but a tactic of controversy.

4   The Trinity as the Logic of God

Andrews Norton and Nathaniel W. Taylor

I

Among those who watched the developing controversy with greatest concern for the "moral tendency" of Christian doctrine was Andrews Norton (1763-1853), Dexter Professor of Sacred Literature at Harvard. Norton was descended from a long line of New England ministers, and upon his graduation from Harvard he read theology under Henry Ware, Sr. His venture into the parish ministry lasted only a few weeks before he turned to an academic career, first as librarian and then as professor at Harvard. He read widely in contemporary German scholarship and sought to appropriate the rise of biblical criticism for the liberal cause. By virtue of his marriage to the daughter of Samuel Eliot, he was able to resign his Harvard post in 1830 and devote his full attention to writing his monumental *Evidences of the Genuiness of the Gospels,* living independently on the income from a large inheritance that supported his family at their gracious "Shady Hill" estate near Harvard Yard.[1]

Norton's entry into the controversy came in the summer issue of *The Christian Disciple* for 1819 with his "Review of Stuart's Letters to Channing." Norton did not share Channing's distaste for controversy, and he immediately took to the offensive by charging that Stuart was attacking persons and not doctrines. Such personal attacks were most uncharitable because anyone ought to be able to publish his views that the trinity was a scandal to the Christian faith, without suffering personal affronts. In Norton's opinion, *The Panoplist,* the chief vehicle for conservative views, was little more than a ragsheet, a channel of "falsehood and scurrility, as we should expect to find only in the vilest newspaper of a profligate political faction."[2] Norton was particularly aroused by Stuart's "loose and inconsistent" principles of interpretation, and he advises him both "that the agreement was not so great as Prof. Stuart supposed" and that he had better settle his principles of interpretation before writing again on the subject. As to Stuart's formulation of the doctrine of the trinity, Norton finds that it sinks behind a veil of inconsistencies and self-contradictory statements that are covered by the single word "distinctions." Not only did Stuart fail to establish the threefold distinction in the Godhead on the basis of Scripture, he had so confused the issue of the personality of the Son that "we cannot well know with what we are contending in opposing Prof. Stuart's doctrine of the trinity."[3]

Norton pursued these arguments in the next issue of the *Disciple*. His article was entitled "A Statement of Reasons for not Believing the Doctrines of Trinitarians Concerning the Nature of God and the Person of Christ." The article was an immediate success, and a number of years later, at the urging of "a highly esteemed friend," Norton expanded it into a book which reached its twelfth and final edition in 1880. His strictures against the doctrine of the trinity are complete and uncompromising: this doctrine is "part of a system which has been substituted for true religion." Spurred by a sense of the progressive unfolding of truth and the subsequent elevating of character formed by that truth, Norton vindicated the need to give a statement of reasons against false doctrines. Nothing less than the nature of Christianity is at stake, and the "great truths of religion" are to be repristinated by a calm application of enlightened hermeneutical principles. The age of enlightened men simply cannot afford to maintain the accumulated theological "rubbish" of the past. The role of religion in society is to lift men's minds above the pale of superstition and their spirits beyond the threat of infidelity. If the role of religion is to make men better, of what possible value is the doctrine of the trinity? It is out of a deep moral conviction of the damage done to society by the propagation of false doctrine that Norton gives his *Statement of Reasons* for not believing the trinity. The alternative was the loss of Christianity and the continued spread of Deism and infidelity.[4]

Norton presses the charge that the doctrine of the trinity in its many guises is "essentially incredible," a doctrine that clearly contradicts the great and fundamental truth of the unity of God. He distinguishes no less than five prevailing forms of the doctrine, and he concludes that each is simply a case of three Gods. The conclusion is inescapable that "three persons each equally possessing divine attributes, are three Gods."[5] Equally incredible and unscriptural is the notion of a hypostatic union of human and divine natures in Christ. "Who defends these doctrines must do it as an unbeliever and not a Christian," for they are absurd and "revelation from God cannot teach absurdities."[6] Nortion is convinced that the trinity and the divinity of Christ are philosophical corruptions of the New Testament resulting from the early Fathers' too easy accomodation to the pressures of culture and history. A "fatal conjuction of Christianity with Platonism resulted in distortions of the New Testament, and only now are we able to recover from these distortions by means of biblical criticism. Norton was convinced that the historical reliability of the Bible was to be trusted much more than the historical unreliability of creeds and dogmas. The eternal truths of religion may be plucked from their historical context like brands from a burning fire, and there was simply no way that the trinity could be numbered among those essentials of true religion. The trinity got caught in Norton's net of biblical criticism and was filtered out of the pure faith as "both unscriptural and irrational."

Norton also undertook an explanation of language, which he described as a very "ambiguous" tool, an imperfect instrument for the expression of thought. Each word has a history and therefore a variety of meanings—a fact Trinitarians have conveniently chosen to overlook. Words may be used literally, figuratively, or emotively, and the art of interpretation consists in uncovering the meaning intended by an author in a given age by recreating the historical environment out of which he wrote, the character of the writer, his habits of thought and feeling, his style, the extent of his knowledge and so forth. "But this principle, which is adapted unconsciously in the interpretation of all other writings, has been grossly disregarded in the interpretation of Scripture."[7] With this principle in mind, it is possible that some passages of Scripture will bear a trinitarian interpretation. But is this the interpretation intended by the writer? Norton was convinced that in no instance could a trinitarian interpretation be ascribed to a text without violence to the intended meaning and to fundamental principles of interpretation.

Further, to call the trinity an incomprehensible mystery is a slight of hand that is not permissible. Words are human instruments for the expression of human ideas, and whatever propositions we make must have a meaning that is comprehensible.

> Language cannot be formed into propositions having a meaning, which meaning is not, in itself considered, fully to be comprehended. . . .When it is affirmed that the Father is God, and the Son is God, and the Holy Ghost is God; and yet there are not three Gods but one God; no words can more clearly convey any meaning than those propositions express the meaning that there are three existences of whom the attributes of God may be predicated, and yet there is only one existence of whom the attributes of God may be predicated. But this is not an incomprehensible mystery; it is plain nonsense.[8]

The doctrine of the trinity was forcing a new theory of language which would be carved out of several sources and reach its fullest expression in Horace Bushnell. For the moment, however, biblical criticism held sway in the work of both Andrews Norton and Moses Stuart. The doctrine of the trinity was the ground upon which biblical criticism would test its wings, and the bulk of Norton's *Statement* consisted of explanations of passages of the New Testament adduced by Trinitarians. Perhaps Norton's work is less a shift in position attempting "to establish the logical absurdity of the Trinitarian theology rather than continuing Channing's discussion about the nature of biblical authority,"[9] than it is an enlargement of the liberal position by applying principles of interpretation to a specific issue, i.e., the doctrine of the trinity. In any event, Harvard and Andover were further apart than ever, and instead of providing a common ground for discussion, biblical criticism drove the two sides to firm entrenchment of their positions.

II

The life of Yale College and the Connecticut Valley in the late eighteenth and early nineteenth centuries was dominated by the powerful presence of Timothy Dwight (1752-1817). Especially after his elevation to the presidency of Yale, Dwight was in a position to spearhead the battle against Deism and infidelity and to guide the course of evangelical religion. His powerful chapel sermons at Yale left their impact upon a whole generation of undergraduates, and later, when they were collected, they ran to four volumes of *Theology Explained*.[10]

Within this comprehensive system of doctrines and duties, the doctrine of the trinity emerges after discussions of the nature of God, the divinity of Christ, and the personality of the Holy Spirit. Unlike most of his contemporaries, Dwight documented evidence for the trinity from ancient Jewish and heathen, as well as Christian, sources. He searched the Old Testament, the works of Philo and Rabbi Judah, and in each instance he uncovered evidence for God as three in one. Among the heathens, the Hindoos (with "Brama, Veeshnu and Seeva"), the Persians, Greeks (Plato's the God, the Mind, the Soul), the Egyptians, Romans, Chinese, and native Americans (the Iroquois) all displayed "the wonderful manner in which God has diffused and perpetuated, the evidence of this doctrine throughout seccessive periods of time."[11]

However, these evidences are merely the roots of the trinity; the true trinity comes to life in the revelation of Scripture. How fully to explicate the trinity escapes Dwight, however, for "the doctrine plainly lies wholly out of the course, I think I may say out of the reach of human thought."[12] With respect to the trinity, then, theology is not so much "explained" as defended, and Dwight's real interest is in stemming those tendencies towards Unitarianism that he has discerned among eastern New Englanders. He repeats what was to become a tiresome plea that Unitarians misrepresent the Trinitarian position by labeling it tritheism. "The admission of three infinitely perfect Beings does not at all imply the existence of more Gods than one."[13] Perhaps Dwight was convinced that the weight of his asserting this point made it so, but few Unitarians were convinced by fiat. He also repeats the orthodox litany about the inadequacy of language, especially the word "person," which no Trinitarian supposed "conveys an adequate idea of the thing here intended—much less that, when it is applied to God, it denotes the same thing, as when applied to created beings."[14] He admits that "the sense in which they are three, and yet one, we do not, and cannot understand," but he falls back on what seemed to be an irrefutable argument that "still we understand the fact; and on this fact depend the truth, and meaning of the whole Scriptural system."[15] Who could argue with facts? The trinity is an indisputable fact which could be understood with a minimum of difficulty and about which argument is futile. The distance from Edwards at this point is considerable, for whatever the deficiencies of Edwards's doctrine of the trinity, he did not advance it with a kind of revelational positivism that said take it or leave it.

Dwight did not wish, however, to drain all mystery from this doctrine, for behind the fact lies the thing itself—where one encounters mystery and the unintelligible. With this distinction of fact and thing clearly in mind, "the utmost amount of all that can be said against the doctrine of the Trinity, is that it is mysterious or inexplicable."[16] This objection, however, is harmless because there are many mysteries about man and many more about God. Dwight was pleased to have his cake and eat it too, for the trinity held together both facticity and mystery in one common sense whole.

Dwight remained primarily the tactician rather than the dogmatician of the trinity, concerned more to counter emerging Unitarian charges than to offer a comprehensive presentation of the trinity. His concern was more for the mode of controversy than for its content, and although he perceived the trinity to be the keystone of Christian theology, he chose not to develop the doctrine beyond rudimentary assertions that involved little risk and could be defended with ease. He was satisfied that his explanation of the trinity was sufficient to dismiss Unitarianism as a halfway house to infidelity and as a movement small enough to be inconsequential anyway.

III

Among the Yale undergraduates who fell most decisively under the persuasive influence of Dwight, was Nathaniel William Taylor (1786-1858), who remained for several years after his graduation in the Dwight household both to serve as the president's secretary and to study theology. A handsome, brilliant, and imposing figure, Taylor was ordained and called as Moses Stuart's successor to the prestigious Center Church in New Haven in 1812, where he remained for ten years and distinguished himself as one of New England's most powerful preachers. When it became increasingly clear that Connecticut Congregationalists would have to carve out their existence between Old Calvinist Presbyterians and Unitarians, the move was made to establish a separate theological seminary at Yale. This effort was given added impetus by the general movement of theological education from parsonages of individual ministers to schools with separate theological faculties. In 1822, Yale invited the triumverate of Chauncy A. Goodrich, Eleazer T. Fitch, and Nathaniel W. Taylor to establish a faculty of divinity. Taylor assumed the post of Dwight Professor of Didactic Theology the same year and remained in this position until declining health forced him to retire in 1857. The "New Haven theology" that emerged has been repeatedly analyzed in terms of its predominate anthropological interests in the nature of the will and original sin. Accordingly, Taylor is remembered for his comprehensive lectures *On Moral Government*, while his essay on the trinity has been all but forgotten.[17]

Taylor was restless with the Andover defense of orthodoxy. Stuart had not held up well under Channing's attack, and he was convinced that Stuart's colleague at Andover, Leonard Woods, had set the orthodox cause back fifty years.[18] If Unitarianism was to be curbed, it would have to be met not only with more precise statements about the nature of man, but also with a more clear and concise statement of the doctrine of the trinity. In its present form, Taylor claims, "the proposition that there are three persons in one God, in the ordinary signification of the terms, is absurd."[19] This assertion was not exactly designed to cheer the hearts of the orthodox, but Taylor was far from finished. Sounding more like a rationalist than the rationalists themselves, Taylor lashes out at those who call the trinity a revealed doctrine and then hide behind the mask of mystery. The powers of logic can in fact penetrate the trinity, and no one is asked to believe what cannot be understood. Clearly, if a doctrine is revealed it can be understood and taught—otherwise what is the point of revelation? A revealed truth such as the trinity is a *fact* that can be understood and not a mystery that is incomprehensible. If Trinitarians could only learn to use language with greater precision, they could bring to expression such truths without being charged with absurdity. The doctrine of the trinity, then, is primarily a problem of language, and the need is to clarify the laws of usage so that men of common sense may arrive at a "settled opinion" regarding this important doctrine.

A survey of Trinitarian thought in New England from Emmons to Stuart is brought forward by Taylor to demonstrate the consequences of the misuse of language. Of Emmons, "it is difficult to say anything positively," and Stuart's discussion of "distinctions" is so shot through with incongruities that it is useless. If one posits a distinction in the Godhead, one must have the courage to go ahead and describe it, otherwise one is employing words without meaning. Trinitarians must make it very clear that when they use such terms as "distinctions," "Persons," and "Being," they are using language in a "peculiar yet authorized import." Such terms are turned from their common ordinary usage to a modified and peculair usage that is governed by laws of interpretation. If, for example, the ordinary usage of the term "person" is imported into discussions of the trinity, then Tritheism, Unitarianism, or absurdity is unavoidable. The trinity is an exigency of language, and Taylor is prepared to demonstrate what he means:

God is one being, in such a modified sense of the term as to include three persons in such a modified sense of the terms, that, by his tri-personality, or by the three persons of his Godhead he is qualified, in a corresponding modified sense, for three distinct, personal, divine forms of phenomenal action; or thus, God, in a modified use of the language, is one being in three persons, qualified by the three persons of the Godhead for three distinct, divine, personal forms of phenomenal action.[20]

Taylor was convinced beyond doubt that the modification of words by restricting or extending their usage would give the language of the trinity an obvious, intelligible, and consistent meaning. Such modification in the meaning of words is warranted only for good and sufficient reason, but surely with the terms "Being" and "Person," as applied to the trinity, there can be no question. Language must be adapted to the nature of the subject at hand and modified according to the exigency of the case. Curiously, Taylor has told us that God is one being in some modified sense of the term, but he does not go on to say precisely what the nature of this modification is. Probably he failed to do that because he was unsure himself what form the modification would take. In any event, he was so anxious to escape the horns of Tritheism, Unitarianism, and absurdity that he wound the doctrine of the trinity into such technical verbiage that only a new theory of language which was forthcoming in Horace Bushnell could rescue the trinity.

For the moment, however, Taylor spun the web of truth as he saw it, and he was prepared at this point to hazard a definition of the trinity: "that God is one being in such an extended sense of the terms, as to involve three persons in such a restricted sense of the terms, that by his Godhead, he is qualified in a corresponding restricted sense, for three distinct, personal, divine forms of phenomenal action."[21] Without these expansions and restrictions of language, literalism results and, of course, Unitarians have then won the day. But Taylor is interested in undermining the Unitarian pretense that such conceptions as the tripersonality of God are *a priori* impossible. By taking the common, ordinary, phenomenal conception of being derived from our own consciousness as the only and universal conception of being, Unitarians conclude that this negates the possibility of tripersonality in the Godhead. In the ordinary sense of language, Unitarians are right, but in the modified and extended usage of language they are wrong, because in the case of the trinity we have to do not with phenomenal conceptions but with revelation. The Unitarian does not know as much as he pretends, for it is impossible to affirm *a priori* that God cannot exist as three persons in one being. Did this answer the Unitarian charge that Trinitarianism was contradictory and absurd? In Taylor's judgment it certainly did, for he was convinced that this flourish of logic had silenced Unitarian objections and deflated Unitarian pretensions to know absolutely what God can and cannot do. Reason has its limitations, and revelation may provide another way of looking at things.

Having demonstrated to the satisfaction of rational men that failing to understand *how* three persons can exist as one being is not the same as saying that this *cannot* be done, Taylor proceeds to build upon this base as a presumption for the truth of the trinity. Neither reason nor revelation furnishes evidence against the doctrine of the trinity if one understands that language may be extended or restricted in usage. The very nature of revelation demands this, for language grows with God's progressive revelation. For example, when the time came for an unfolding of the great work of redemption, further knowledge of God was given and with it an extension in the meaning of the term "being" to even more explicit tripersonal usage. Redemption proceeds according to a Trinitarian plan, and the moral government of God goes into effect through the trinity by way of the atoning work of the second person and the sanctifying work of the third person.

Taylor is now ready to tackle the center of the controversy: the manner in which language is used in the Scripture respecting the mode of the divine subsistence and the person of Christ. Certain that the language of Scripture "is not characterized by the authorized obscurity of enigma, of allegory, or prophetic annunciation, or of typical or symbolic representation. . .that it bears none of the peculiar marks of figurative or metaphorical language,"[22] his Scottish common sense realism leads Taylor to assert that the language of the Bible is that of plain men of common life which is easily understood by honest simplicity. At this point he pronounces a plague on the houses of both Unitarians and Trinitarians, for each appeals to inspiration as the foundation of scriptural use of language. But such appeals settle nothing, for language is just as meaningless if improperly employed by an inspired writer as by an uninspired writer: "You do not ask first whether the writers are inspired but how they *use* language."[23] Language is the reality with which we have most directly to deal, and simply appealing to the inspiration of the Scripture to establish or to deny the doctrine of the trinity or the divinity of Christ is insufficient. Inspiration does little to clarify the meaning of language; clarity can be achieved only by sound hermeneutical principles. In short, Taylor's essay was an effort to formulate a doctrinal rebuttal to Unitarianism and to rally support among his followers. Revivalism might be one suitable technique to counter the Unitarian challenge, but

> The history of the progress of Unitarianism in this country, as well as some recent limited tendencies toward it, clearly indicate the necessity, not only of explaining the doctrine of the trinity, of insisting on the possibility of its truth, and of removing all presumptions against its truth, but of showing how the peculiar language of the Scripture is fully accounted for and authorized in view of the nature of the subject circumstances of the case; on what principles such peculiar language ought to be interpreted, and what, when interpreted on these principles, is its actual meaning.[24]

He then rather lamentably asks, "what advocate of the trinity has ever attempted to show what the changes are, and on what principles of usage they are authorized, and having done this, to fix the precise import of the language in its changed and yet authorized use?" With equal lament he answers his inquiry simply and directly: "No Trinitarian has ever tried this. . . ."[25]

Taylor's love of logic and clear definitions convinced him that others would yield to his presentation of the trinity under the irresistible force of logical proofs. His love of free inquiry was a source of irritation to the orthodox, but it was also a source of inspiration to at least one of his students who formulated a new theory of language whereby the trinity was less a matter of logic and more a gift to the imagination.

5   The Trinity as the Language of God

Horace Bushnell

I

The life of Horace Bushnell spanned nearly three quarters of the nineteenth century, and his career as pastor and author reflects the changing currents and complexities of the era. He was born in April of 1802, at Bantam, Connecticut, to a farming family whose sacrifices enabled his matriculation as a student at Yale College in 1823.[1] Bushnell distinguished himself as a student and athlete, and as an undergraduate he fell under the particular spell of Samuel Taylor Coleridge's *Aids to Reflection*. Upon graduation he tried his hand at both teaching and journalism before returning to Yale in 1829, as both a law student and tutor. A revival that swept through the College in 1831 left its impact on Bushnell, and he enrolled in the Yale Divinity School the same year. Graduating in 1833, he accepted a call to the North Congregational Church in Hartford, Connecticut, a position he held until 1859, when he was forced by failing health to resign. He declined offers of the presidency of both Middlebury College and the University of California at Berkeley, in whose founding he had played a prominent role, to devote himself to his pastoral duties and his extensive writing. The range of his interests encompassed not only theological issues, but a concern for the West, a fear of papalism, a condemnation of slavery, an insightful interpretation of the Civil War, and an appreciation for New England history and lore.

During Bushnell's student years at Yale, Nathaniel W. Taylor held sway with the New Haven Theology. As we have seen, Taylor's discussion of the trinity was too technical and involved to advance trinitarian theory much, if at all. However, his attempt to define the trinity impressed upon Bushnell the necessity for a new theory of language if the doctrine of the trinity was to be rescued from the thicket of dogmatic theology. The clues for this reformulation of language came not from Taylor but from another of Bushnell's Yale professors, Josiah Willard Gibbs. Gibbs was a distinguished philologist, well acquainted with German scholarship and sensitive to the development of words founded

> on the analogy and correlation of the physical and intellectual worlds. . .Words which originally belonged to the world of sense, and denoted sensible objects, operations and relations are transferred by a metaphor depending on a perceived analogy, to the world of intellect to express mental objects, operations and relations.[2]

Bushnell welcomed this discovery of the centrality of metaphor and coupled it with a reading of *Aids to Reflection* by Samuel Taylor Coleridge, from whom he learned the value of intuitive knowledge.

In the fall of 1839, Bushnell was invited to address the Porter Rhetorical Society of Andover Seminary. He miscalculated by a week the amount of time he had to prepare the address, and he was forced to lock himself in his study for a day before departing for Andover the next morning. The focus of the address was the relation between form and truth, as well as the nature of language as a vehicle to mirror the truth. The address was entitled "Revelation," and in it Bushnell sought to establish the case that language itself is a revelation of God by which truth is communicated to man. Words are merely the forms which embody the truth; they are not themselves the truth. "I say every truth must have its images or metaphors whereby it may be shown."[3] Truth itself remains invisible behind the forms, but revelation offers to the mind of man figures and images, allegories and paradoxes, that embody the truth. Bushnell illustrates this point by speaking of the three persons of the trinity as the forms which outwardly dramatize the truth of the divine nature, and he suggests that "the doctrine of the trinity will be settled when it is ascertained just how much of this threefold and outwardly contradictory representation is due to the linguistic necessity of the case."[4] The address was never printed in full, but it indicates that early in his career Bushnell was disturbed by the problem of the relation between language, revelation, and the doctrine of the trinity. He reflected on the address in a letter to his wife several days later: "I said some things very cautiously in regard to the trinity which, perhaps, will make a little breeze. If so I shall not feel much upset. I have been thinking lately that I *must* write and publish the whole truth on these subjects as God has permitted me to see it."[5]

It took nine years of spiritual discontent and groping before Bushnell was permitted to see the "whole truth," but on a February morning in 1848, when his wife asked, "What have you seen?" he replied, "The gospel."[6] Later this same year he was invited to deliver commencement addresses at Andover, Yale, and Harvard, and these were collected and introduced with a premilinary "Dissertation on Lanugage as Related to Thought and Spirit." Published under the title *God in Christ,* the book was destined to stir more than "a little breeze."

Bushnell became increasingly skeptical of the ability of words to transplant ideas directly from one mind to another and thereby to establish certain fixed and eternal truths to which all men of reason would give their assent. In his opinion, the problem of language is vastly more complicated, and misconceptions about its nature and capacities have plunged theology into endless methodological confusion. A sanguine trust in language and logic has led theology to the mistaken notion that such matters as the trinity can be expressed in definition and dogma. But the issue is not so simple, for language must be viewed as a human product that is living and not reducible to immobile forms or "wooden blocks." The capacity for language is a unique human instinct by which the outward world is linked to thought. Echoing the teaching of Josiah Gibbs, Bushnell writes, "all things out of sense get their names in language through signs and objects in sense that have some mysterious correspondence or analogy, by which they are prepared beforehand to serve as signs or vehicles of the spiritual things to be expressed."[7] There is an analogy between the physical and the spiritual, between things and thoughts: "There is a *logos* in the forms of things, by which they are prepared to serve as types or images of what is inmost in our souls. . . .In one word, the outer world, which envelopes our being, is itself language, the power of all language."[8]

Bushnell applied this theory to theological language, arguing that because of the limitations of language, theological terms can never represent truth as it is in itself. Since words are rooted in the world of the senses from which they receive their form, there is an element of "form" latent in all thought, such that when by way of metaphor words move from things to thought, they do not do so without remainder. "Words, then, I answer, are legitimately used as the signs of thoughts to be expressed. They do not literally convey or pass over a thought of one mind into another. . . They are only hints or images."[9] In the case of theological language, the problem is compounded, and objectivity remains impossible. Why? Because words used in theological discourse are not only imprecise, "they always affirm something which is false or contrary to the truth intended. They impute *form* to that which really is out of form."[10] The distinction between form and truth, then, becomes a much more delicate matter than New England theology ever suspected. Failure to recognize this fact will mean only that the abortive quest for an objective or scientific theology will continue among theologians who mistakenly find an immediate correspondence between words and truth.

Is theology therefore to wither in silence and despair? Not if it will cease its logic-chopping and system-building and come to appreciate the truth as expressed in metaphor and paradox. Theology must cease treating words as beasts of burden and forcing language to answer purposes that are against its nature. The failure of dogma is not the failure of language, for God comes to expression in language, in the *Logos*, in metaphor. There is need, however, for a different theological method whereby the truth is not pulled into analytic distinctions and definitions that seek to "think out" the Gospel. Rather theology receives the truth as it presents itself to us through the imagination in the forms of images, figures, symbols, and metaphors. In short, the truth is not that which we find by definition and dogma, but that which find us by poetry and metaphor. It is this theory of language which informs Bushnell's prolonged reflections upon the doctrine of the trinity.

The Yale commencement of 1848 provided an ideal context for a distinguished alumnus, now pastor of the North Church in Hartford, to deliver his *"Concio ad Clerum: A Discourse on the Divinity of Christ."* After citing ten marks of Christ's divinity, Bushnell moves quickly to a discussion of two subjects of long-standing controversy between Congregationalists and Unitarians: the person of Christ and the trinity. His dissatisfaction with both parties is made abundantly clear, as he hopes that "we may be induced to let go a trinity that mocks our reason, and a unity that freezes our hearts, and return to the simple Father, Son, and Holy Ghost of the Scriptures and the apostolic fathers."[11] The prevailing attempts of orthodoxy to state the doctrine of the trinity are all equally disastrous, and "they only confuse their understanding and call their confusion faith." Such criticism was not designed to win the applause of the General Association of Connecticut in attendence at the commencement on that August morning, but Bushnell was far from finished. Unitarianism had arisen as a necessary reaction "to clear away the rubbish that speculation had accummulated," and as he surveyed the scene he could find only "signs of mental confusion" everywhere. In short, New England orthodoxy's doctrine of the trinity was quite unorthodox; it threatened the divinity of Christ.

Bushnell then proceeds to rehearse this history of doctrinal confusion, including an attack on Nathanael Emmons's view of three consciousnesses, wills, and understandings in the interior nature of the Godhead. No one can assert this view "and still have any intelligent meaning in his mind, when he asserts that they are yet one person. . . .When he does it, his words will of necessity be only substitutes for sense."[12] As for presentations of the trinity coming out of Andover,

> the class of teachers who protest over the word *persons*, declaring that they mean only a *threefold distinction*, cannot show that there is really a hair's breadth of difference between their doctrine and the doctrine asserted by many of the later Unitarians. . .When they use the term *person*, they mean not a person, but a certain indefinite and indefinable distinctions. The later Unitarians, meantime, are found asserting that God is present in Christ, in a mysterious and peculiar communication of his being, so that he is the living embodiment and express image of God. If now, the question is raised, wherein does the indefinable *distinction* of one differ from the mysterious and peculiar *communication* of the other, or how does it appear that there is any difference, there is no living man, I am quite sure, who can invent an answer. . . .If anyone endeavors to relieve his position by declaring that he only means distinction by the word persons, he then flies into darkness and negation for his comfort, and there he may be left.[13]

The influence of Schleiermacher becomes evident as Bushnell begins to construct his own views of the trinity. Of special importance at this point is his reluctance to probe the interior nature of the Godhead and his unwillingness to say anything about the immanent trinity.

> The trinity we seek will be a trinity that results of necessity from the revelation of God to man. I do not undertake to fathom the interior being of God, and tell how it is composed. That is a matter too high for me, and, I think, for us all. I only insist that assuming the strictest unity and even simplicity of God's nature, he could not be efficiently or sufficiently revealed to us without evolving a trinity of persons such as we meet in the Scriptures. These persons or personalities are the *dramatis personae* of revelation, and their reality is measured by what of infinity they convey in these finite forms. As such, they bear on the one hand, a relation to God, who is to be conveyed or imported into knowledge; on the other they are related to our human capacities and wants, being that presentation of God which is necessary to make him a subject of thought, or bring him within the discourse of reason; that also which is necessary to produce mutuality or terms of conversableness, between us and him, and pour his love most effectually into our feeling.[14]

This passage is important both for an understanding of the charges of Sabellianism against Bushnell and for an appreciation of the Puritan heritage which shaped his thinking. Only recently have efforts been made to rescue him from the hands of those who interpreted him primarily in light of the Romantic tradition through Coleridge. "It is true that Bushnell was significantly influenced by the romantic movement, but it is equally true that both his epistemology and his gospel message are fundamentally rooted in the Puritan tradition."[15] This influence becomes evident in his struggles toward a mature statement of the doctrine of the trinity. Increasingly, for Bushnell, the trinity is that by which relationality and "conversableness" with God are attained, through which God may "pour his love most effectually into our feeling." Also, although it is difficult to establish any direct link between Edwards's treatises on the trinity and Bushnell's thought, the influence of Edwards is present in the sense that, for both, the trinity is a medium of revelation to intellect and feeling. Further, for both men the trinity is that which most fully reveals the glory of God and the plentitude of His being.

The results of Bushnell's reflections upon the nature of language begin to appear at this point in his discussion of the trinity. The trinity, he claims, is one of those paradoxical devices of revelation which does not present us with God fully unmasked, but plays upon our imagination with "infinite repugnances and contrarities." Thus, with the trinity and "in whatever thing God appears or is revealed, there will be something that misrepresents, as well as something that represents Him."[16] Since the last boundary of God is never seen, we must remain content with those instruments of revelation by which God has accommodated himself to finite reason and affection. This of necessity involves imprecision and inexactitude, for the mode of God's self-communication is by incarnation and trinity; these are not static definitions but dynamic realities. The trinity has life: the life of God in Christ and of the Spirit in man.

It remained, however, to work out the relationship between the incarnation and the trinity, and at this point Bushnell asserts that prior to the incarnation "there has been no appearance of trinity in the revelations God has made of his being; but just here—whether as resulting from the incarnation or as implied in it, we are not informed—a threefold personality or impersonation of God begins to offer itself to view."[17] Bushnell's reluctance to probe the immanent trinity forces him in the direction of a trinity developed in time. His language is very cautious, and he avoids saying that the trinity did not exist before the incarnation, he states only that there were no revelations of it prior to the incarnation. He is equally reluctant to probe the interior nature of the person of Christ on the grounds that such an investigation is fruitless. The attempt to make absolutes out of relatives had led in the case of the doctrine of the trinity to reading distinctions back into the Godhead, resulting in tritheism. In the case of the person of Christ, interior probing led to severing the unity of the two natures into a virtual Nestorianism. In both instances, New England theology missed the symbolic importance of these doctrines, and therefore "we throw away all the solvents of the incarnation and the trinity that are given us, and then complain of our difficulties."[18] Bushnell then concludes:

> I will only say that the trinity or the three persons, are given to me for the sake of their external expression, not for the internal investigation of their contents. . . .They must have their reality to me in what they express as the wording forth of God. Perhaps I shall come nearest to the simple, positive idea of the trinity here maintained, if I call it an *instrumental trinity*, and the persons *instrumental persons.* There may be more in them than this, which let others declare when they find it."[19]

The trinity, then, is primarily God's instrumental "wording forth" of Himself; it is the "grammatical form" by which God is brought to our experience and knowledge. Again, it is his theory of language that lies behind Bushnell's conviction that it was necessary for God to "three" Himself into history in order to reveal himself to man. The trinity is God's play upon the imagination of man, far richer than a lifeless Unitarian unity or sterile orthodox distinctions. The trinity is a dynamic affair, and the language by which it is spoken of must be no less dynamic.

II

The publication of Bushnell's *God in Christ* created a dispute that was to drag on for five years within Connecticut Congregationalism. The Association of Fairfield West was particularly active in assailing Bushnell's views, and he defended himself against charges of heterodoxy in a subsequent publication entitled *Christ in Theology*. The wider ecclesiastical controversy need not detain us here, but the refinements in Bushnell's doctrine of the trinity are of interest because in the interim between the publication of *God in Christ* and *Christ in Theology* he studied with some care the history of the doctrine of the trinity. Bushnell admitted elsewhere to his distaste for research, and at least once he was accused of writing first and researching later.[20] But the fruits of his efforts are evident, and he emerges more confident than ever in his position: "I hope therefore, it will not be suspected that I am anxious in the historic references I make, to establish a repute of orthodoxy. I will even declare to you beforehand, that I am not orthodox according to any precise type of orthodoxy that I know. . . ."[21] He proceeds to make it clear that he is going to bypass New England theology in favor of what he conceives to be a more historically orthodox understanding of the trinity.

> I have been examining my relation to proper orthodoxy more carefully of late than I had done before, and the result is a double surprise; in the discovery, first, that I am so much nearer to real orthodoxy than I supposed, and secondly, that New England theology, so called, is so much farther off. . . .I shall be found, in the book you are examining, to stand in much better keeping with the orthodoxy of the Reformation, connected with the previous times and reaching back to the Nicea era, than do the teachers generally and the current opinions of New England.[22]

It is this discovery of the wider stream of Christian doctrine that inspires Bushnell and informs his continued reflections on the trinity.

Reiterating that the trinity eludes the grasp of both logic and dogma, he sought to illustrate his theory of language by application to a specific doctrine. Interestingly enough, it is the doctrine of the eternal generation of the Son that he chooses to examine the relation between language and doctrine. "This doctrine is a good illustration of all the wars of theology," for it provides an excellent instance of a truth corrupted by its forms. By the time this truth reaches the form of dogma, it has degenerated into a barren piece of information that inspires neither thought nor feeling, and not surprisingly then falls into disuse. So in New England theology, "the dogma, unable to live in a form so badly violated, will have gradually perished" because of the failure to go behind the forms and search for the meaning. "We convert forms into abstractions, overlay the abstractions with logical inferences, build the inferences into schemes and systems, and these we call doctrine or theology."[23] This whole theological method needs to be turned around so that we are receptive through insight and intuition to what God expresses to us by form and symbol.

Although exceedingly critical of "the soap-bubble world" of New England theology's system-making, Bushnell nonetheless respects the necessity and value of theology. He is impatient with views of Christianity as a system to be organized into creeds and dogma rather than as a posture of faith receptive to the incarnate mystery of life. The truths of Christianity, including the eternal generation of the Son, the divinity of Christ, and the trinity, are given not as riddles for logic to solve "but simply that God may thus express His own feeling and draw Himself into union with us by an act of accommodation to our human sympathies and capacities."[24] The problem, as Bushnell perceives it, is that New England theology has confused the truth with its forms. If New England theology would only modestly receive the truth of the trinity with a sense that the form in which it is expressed necessarily carries with it an insoluble element of mystery, it would be delivered from the false notion that dogma can fix the form of the trinity permanently. The trinity is rather that which is given to keep the mind alive and restless, teasing and provoking a fertility and growth of thought.

Bushnell is most sensitive to the accusation that he had denied the immanent trinity: "the very tenor of my argument required me *not* to deny it. . . ."[25] He confesses that his language on this topic "might have been more guarded," but the charge is still unjust. The trinity is more than a "dramatic show," more than a development in time, but just how much more Bushnell is reluctant to say. He objects to Stuart's inference that "there must be an 'equivalent threeness' back of the revelation to support its truth." He finds equally objectionable any psychological analogy for the trinity based on a triad in human consciousness. But, "that there is some threefold ground in the divine nature, back of the trinity, I was most careful not to deny." The function of the doctrine of the trinity is not to explore the interior nature of the Godhead, but to prevent either a diminution of God's glory or a loss of God's personality. "And so the Christian trinity, by its two elements of number and personality, holds us to a strain of thought after God, both as *transcending* the categories of our human understanding and as *personal* in his relations and character."[26] The orthodox no less than the Unitarians need to rediscover the doctrine of the trinity as that which protects the magnitude as well as the personhood of God. A more "comprehensive" view would bring together the truth of both sides into a whole that would properly express the transcendence and the immanence of God. Bushnell himself is struggling at this point to balance his view of an instrumental trinity with an ontological ground for it.

In working through this central problem of the doctrine of the trinity, Bushnell is led by his historical studies to a reconsideration of Nicea and specifically the doctrine of the eternal generation of the Son. He turns increasingly away from an "instrumental trinity" to a "trinity of eternal generation," a shift that becomes the interpretive key to Bushnell's mature doctrine of the trinity. He examined the antinomies of the trinity as presented in Scripture and found that the idea of the coinherence (*perichoresis*) or the identity of each person of the Godhead with each other was totally lacking in New England theology. This oversight resulted from attempts to build the doctrine of the trinity upon the being of God while neglecting the act of God. It is God's eternal necessary act of generation that provides the ground for a trinity in which the persons

are each as truly each, as they are each other and different from each. . . .Having rejected the church doctrine of a trinity in act or by eternal generation, and set ourselves to find some possible trinity in God as essence (which plainly is not possible) the whole doctrine of the subject has fallen into the greatest confusion among us.[27]

The charge of provincialism is Bushnell's telling blow against New England orthodoxy, and in many ways it was a highly just criticism.

Yes, I frankly own to you that I accept no prevailing view of trinity now held in New England. If I understand the sense of this doctrine, now prevailing among us, I must dissent from it. . . .The truth is, that what we call orthodoxy on this subject, in New England, is wholly unhistorical—a provincialism, a kind of theological *patois*, quite peculiar to ourselves.[28]

This lack of historical breadth Bushnell attributes in no small part to New England theology's rejection of the doctrine of eternal generation. An incompetent theological method which confused truth with its form discarded the Nicene formulation of eternal generation on the grounds that it necessarily implied a subordination of the Son. "Then going on to ply our logic on the matter of the trinity, with a principle term or element wanting, viz., that which alone makes the truth possible, we run ourselves at once into complications of heresy much to be deplored, because they are complications of real and very pernicious error."[29] The regard with which Bushnell had come to hold the doctrine of eternal generation is immediately apparent: it is "that which alone makes truth possible." This is so because God is essentially pure act, He is "eternally threeing himself" in history. The persons of the trinity are predicable of the Godhead as act, and not as being. But, "ceasing to conceive a trinity of act, we began to assert a trinity of persons in the divine essence itself, which is plain tritheism."[30] Bushnell will later temper his views on this point, but at the moment he is convinced that New England had simply "slidden completely off the basis of historic orthodoxy," and had removed from its doctrine of the trinity "that alone which gave it balance and enabled it to stand. . . ." His heightened respect for the Nicene Creed is evident, and he notes:

the eternal generation is not a matter collateral to the conception of trinity but fundamental to it. . . .Apart from this they knew no trinity. The persons had their personality in these conceptions of eternal generation and eternal procession, and apart from these they were nothing.[31]

To miss this is to turn the doctrine of trinity into "a residual tritheitic compost," by which no man ought to be judged.

Chirst in Theology represents a continued movement in Bushnell's thought from a trinity generated in time as an historical revelation to "the conviction that the conditions and grounds out of which it is generated in time are eternal, and so it is itself eternal."[32] He is moving toward a threeness that is immanent in the Godhead. The finite remains, however, as the

ground of the trinity, or as he says of his view, "instead of beginning trans-
cendentally at a point within the active life of God, it takes a humbler
method, beginning at the consideration of our media and powers of
knowledge, and the conditions under which Infinite Being and Spirit may be
revealed or expressed to us."[33] His mind, however, was in flux, and
sensitive to his own advice about the nature of the trinity, he continued to
search for and remain receptive to alternative forms of expression.

III

Bushnell's continued interest in the trinity is reflected in an article
published in the *New Englander* for November, 1854, entitled "The
Christian Trinity a Practical Truth." The problem of an ontological ground
for the trinity had continued to haunt Bushnell, and he sought now "to
ascend to a point more interior as a ground in the eternity of God, antecedent to the revelation in time."[34] Reflection on the relation of the trinity
to time and eternity led him to the conclusion that the trinity does not come
into being with the incarnation and does not cease to exist once the work of
redemption is accomplished. Here Bushnell shows a greater willingness to
investigate the trinity from the Godhead side as that which expresses and
protects the magnitude of the gospel and the grandeur of God. From the
manward side, the trinity is needed as an accommodation to the mind
and heart of man which best receive God in terms of personality. The loss of
either the magnitude or the personality of God issues in two errors,
pantheism or Unitarianism. Bushnell commends pantheism for its efforts to
protect the infinity of God, but criticizes it for losing the personality of
God. He commends the Unitarians for preserving the relational terms of
personalilty and the Fatherhood of God, but condemns them for reducing
the infinity of God. The importance of the trinity is that it "secures at once
the practical infinity of God and the practical personality of God."[35]

Far from being a "theologic fiction" or a "riddle of the faith," the
trinity expresses the richness of God by a "threefold grammatic
personality." The trinity is a sign that God enters the word-structure of
reality; it is that which brings together nature and the supernatural. God's
economy is twofold, "comprising at one pole an economy of nature, and at
the other, an economy of supernatural grace; requiring, in order to an easy
practical adjustment of our life under it, a twofold conception of God that
corresponds; for which reason the Scripture three are sometimes spoken of
by Calvin and others, as comprising an economic trinity."[36] Bushnell's
opposition to a growing naturalism, expressed fully in his *Nature and the
Supernatural*, may be seen in this essay on the trinity. If nature is the end all
and be all, if Christianity is translated into naturalistic categories, "if the
universal economy included nothing but nature, the single term or

conception *God*, would answer all our necessary uses—so far there would be no discoverable economic need of Trinity."[37] But this is not the case, for there are two orders of being, nature and supernatural, and God is not to be conceived except in terms of this twofold relation to humanity. The trinity alone provides us with a comprehensive method to harmonize the relation of nature and the supernatural. Thus the needs of sinful men and the redemptive power of God's sin-bearing love intersect in the trinity.

The trinity, then, is not merely a matter of words; it is an eternal fact as well as a practical truth. God is triune, not only in revelation but in Himself, and the trinity is not an occasional matter or a voluntary expedient, but an interior necessity. This is a significant move for Bushnell in the direction of classical Trinitarianism, and the conclusion is therefore accurate that "Bushnell's doctrine of the trinity falls completely within the orb of the orthodox faith."[38] Again, it is the doctrine of eternal generation that presses the conclusion that God is "eternally threeing Himself," which does "not mean that God, at some date in His almanac called eternity, begat His Son and sent forth His Holy Spirit, but that in some high sense undefinable, He is datelessly and eternally becoming three, or by a certain inward necessity being accommodated in His action to the categories of finite apprehension. . . ."[39]

Above all, the trinity is a consciousness-expanding experience, a gift to the imagination, and "a vast opening of God to man." Elsewhere, in a remarkable essay on "Our Gospel a Gift to the Imagination," Bushnell repeated his conviction that the trinity is a grand, fundamental, and most practical truth of Christianity. "These three images are God as delivered to the imagination, and the grammatic threeness in which they stand is a truth in metaphor, even as the grammatic personalities are metaphoric and not literal persons; the God-idea, figured under these relativities, obtains, in the resulting mystery, the largest, freshest, liveliest impression possible."[40] So, too, the person of Christ is given to the imagination, and "we can say nothing of Christ so comprehensively adequate as to call Him the metaphor of God; God's last metaphor."[41]

It is not strange that Bushnell's last sermon was preached on I Corinthians 15:28 and further explored the subject of the trinity through "Our Relations to Christ in the Future Life." He was a skilled preacher with an uncanny ability to weave difficult theological questions into a tapestry of intelligibility and practical application within the context of a sermon. Sensing the approaching end of his career, Bushnell notes, "if it should happen that this is the last sermon I am permitted to give, it will not be amiss that, for once, I have preached to myself."[42] His concern is again to demonstrate that the personality and infinity of God are maintained by trinity, that the dimension of depth is saved by this "inherently necessary" accommodation by God to finite minds. There is, then, an anthropological base for the trinity in the needs of man as sinner. But, more decisively, there are reasons, or distinctions in God's own nature, i.e., there are theological justifications for speaking of three persons. There is more to the trinity than the mere instrumentality of revelation; the trinity does not serve just the occasional uses of redemption and then dissolve. The trinity is both a temporal accommodation and an eternal necessity; history and eschatology yield to a triune form.

Again, it is the eternal Sonship of Christ that precludes the evaporation of the trinity. Combating the Jesusology of a popular piety that delivers the dead "safe in the arms of the Master," Bushnell argues that "our relations to Christ, then, in the future life, are to be relations to God in Christ, and never to the Jesus in Christ."[43] Both in time and in eternity, Christ is Son only and always in trinity, and

> it follows that, before creation and before incarnation, God Himself was somehow, or in some sense, Man. He had, that is, an anthropoid nature, which anthropodial nature is a kind of Divine Man-Form or Word, by which he thinks himself, incarnates Himself, and types Himself in his creations.[44]

In this way, a genuine incarnation is secured, because humanity is a character of the eternal Son—who is "the God-Man everlastingly present, integrally present, in trinity before either we or the world began."[45]

It should be clear that throughout his career Bushnell repeatedly turned to the doctrine of the trinity as a mode of adumbrating Christian thought and experience. He did not share the embarrassment of liberalism about the trinity, and he did not join the denigration of the trinity common to the nineteenth century "Jesus of history" school. Similarly, although he acknowledged the importance of Schleiermacher, he did not make the trinity an appendix to his thought or treat it as an unwarranted addition to the faith because it did not explicate the content of Christian self-consciousness. On the contrary, for Bushnell the trinity answered to Christian experience as nothing else could, and his whole understanding of language and revelation is tied to the doctrine of the trinity. Most importantly, though, it was Bushnell's struggles with the doctrine of the trinity that confronted him with his own parochialism and drove him to what was for him an exciting and refreshing discovery of the wider stream of the history of Christian doctrine. It was this search for a usable past, for resources from within not only his immediate historical context, but, more importantly, from the broader spectrum of Christian life and thought that made Bushnell perplexing to his contemporaries and makes him challenging to American theology in the present.

Conclusion

If it is true that one is in danger of losing his soul by denying the trinity and of losing his wits by trying to understand it, then both souls and wits were lost in the period from Edwards to Bushnell. Basically, there was never any question about the unity of God, for all agreed that there is one God. As to the nature of this one God and how he communicates himself to man, however, the divisions of opinion were sharp, and the doctrine of the trinity figured prominently in the search for an adequate theological method and language. The doctrine of the trinity forced discussion on the role of reason, the authority of Scripture, the meaning of history, and the nature of faith and practice. For those who denied the trinity did so on the grounds that it was an embarrassment to reason, a burden to biblical criticism, a matter of mere antiquarian interest and of no practical value.

Those who sought to retain and defend the trinity were forced to demonstrate, first, that it was not irrational. But sorting out the role of reason proved to be not so easy. Defenders of the trinity had no interest in erecting a cult of the unintelligible in order to protect a doctrine of the faith. Faith does not demand the jettisoning of reason, nor does it require the adoption of absurdities. But reason has its boundaries, and the doctrine of the trinity forced a recognition of the limits of reason in a milieu more receptive to its unlimited powers. The trinity was both an exercise in the use of reason and a lesson in the limits of reason. The suggestion that mystery remains as part of human experience and that the trinity is part of the inevitable mystery of God was not embraced with enthusiasm by the age of reason. To a considerable extent, then, the doctrine of the trinity was a battleground between natural and revealed religion, and rather than serving to give unity to reason and faith, the trinity tended to drive the natural and the supernatural further apart.

A crisis of equal magnitude, however was produced by the charge that the doctrine of the trinity was unscriptural. This was a formidable objection that would have to be met with persuasive strength. Biblical criticism became a tool in the hands of the trinity's opponents and defenders alike, as interest focused on this doctrine as a test case for critical scholarship. Just as there was agreement that God is one, and that reason cannot be abrogated, so there was agreement that the Scriptures were an authoritative guide for faith and practice. The crisis, however, was one of interpretation, and the doctrine of the trinity again played a role through a confusion of interpretations derived from commonly applied interpretative principles. Although biblical criticism was hailed as the great unifier, in the end it served just the opposite purpose. As might be suspected, both sides found support for their views in critical evaluations of biblical texts.

The trinity also precipitated a crisis in the uses of tradition and history. Those who denied the trinity argued simply that it was the product of corruption—an abortive doctine that had no place in the faith of the church. While there was agreement that Christianity was an historical faith, there was widespread disagreement on the meaning and uses of history. The church fathers were ransacked for evidence both for and against the trinity, and the history of doctrine faced a crisis of confidence. The conflicts over text and tradition, over the role of creeds and confessions, centered in no small degree on the trinity. For some, the search for a usable past ended in a pile of rubbish; for others, the discovery of the ancient traditions of the church came as a liberation from the parochialism of the present.

The doctrine of the trinity finally seemed to fail the test of practicality, which was perhaps the ultimate criterion in an increasingly utilitarian society. There seemed to be no connection between the doctrine of the trinity and the life of faith, and one of the most damaging charges against it was that it served only to distract the worship of the believer. Coupled to this was the argument from "moral tendency," which claimed that such doctrines as the trinity served only to cripple faith and to produce an undesirable moral effect in those who hold them. A defense of the doctrine of the trinity required, then, that it be taken from isolation and restored both as an operative doctrine within systematic theology, and as a meaningful expression of human experience. The doctrine of the trinity had lost touch with its roots in experience and practice, sacrificing itself to theory and study. The problem was how to speak of religious realities which cannot be expressed only as a doctrine, but which are experienced in the life of faith. The trinity speaks to both the head and the heart, to thought and emotion, and it was this rediscovery that freed the trinity to become again a practical truth. There is a wholeness to the self, even as there is a unity behind the multiplicity of human experience, and the trinity seeks to express this quest. Although the trinity transcends human thought it does not reside in the realm of the esoteric, but may serve to illuminate experience and give it meaning.

The doctrine of the trinity, therefore, does not deserve the benign neglect it has received at the hands of American religious historiography. It figured prominently in theological discussions among major figures in the period as they sought a way to express the self-revelation of God to man. Moralism, on the one side, and creedalism, on the other, threatened to sap the doctine of the trinity of its vitality. But there were ongoing attempts to call upon the doctrine of the trinity to bring together the transcendent and the immanent, to express God in His essence and in His revelation, and to set forth the paradox of time and eternity, the absolute and the relative, unity and diversity, being and personality. The story of this struggle and of

Conclusion

the changing conceptions of the trinity from the mid-eighteenth to the mid-nineteenth century in American theology is a tradition worthy of the historian of doctrine. Despite much clamor and trivia that accompanied it, the overall scholarly and intellectual character of this movement make it an outstanding chapter in American religious life and thought.

Notes

Notes to Chapter 1

[1] Jonathan Edwards, "Dissertation on the End for which God Created the World," *Works of President Edwards*, Reprint of Worcester Edition, 4 vols. (New York: Jonathan Leavitt and John F. Trow, 1843-44), 2:210. Biographical information on Edwards may be found in the *Dictionary of American Biography* (New York: 1929), 6:30-37; hereafter referred to as *DAB*; Sereno E. Dwight, *The Life of President Edwards in the Works of President Edwards*. vol. 1; Ola Winslow, *Jonathan Edwards, 1703-1758* (New York: Collier Books, 1961).

[2] Edwards, "Dissertation on the End," p. 253.

[3] Jonathan Edwards, *Miscellanies*, no. 362. These *Miscellanies* are drawn from *The Philosophy of Jonathan Edwards from his Private Notebooks*. ed. Harvey G. Townsend (Eugene, Oregon: University of Oregon Press, 1955). See also Appendix I in *Exercises Commemorating the Two-Hundredth Anniversary of the Birth of Jonathan Edwards*, ed., E. C. Smyth (Andover: 1904), pp. 3-60.

[4] *Miscellanies*, no. 1082; see also no. 1218.

[5] Edwards, "Dissertation on the End," p. 259.

[6] George P. Fisher, ed., *An Unpublished Essay of Edwards on the Trinity* (New York: Chas. Scribner's Sons, 1903), p. xv. This essay, along with Edwards's *Treatise on Grace* and his *Observations Concerning the Trinity and the Covenant of Redemption*, has been edited and introduced by Paul Helm (London: James Clarke & Co., Ltd., 1971).

[7] Ibid., pp. 80-81.

[8] Ibid., p. 94.

[9] Ibid., pp. 110-11.

[10] Oliver Wendel Holmes, "Jonathan Edwards," *International Review* 9 (1880): 125.

[11] Edwards A. Park, "Remarks of Jonathan Edwards on the Trinity," *Bibliotheca Sacra* 38 (April, 1881): 367.

[12] Jonathan Edwards, *Observations Concerning the Scripture Oeconomy of the Trinity and Covenant of Redemption*, ed., Egbert C. Smyth (New York: 1880), p. 24.

[13] Ibid., pp. 21-22.

[14] Ibid., p. 27.

[15] Ibid., p. 56. See also Edwards's sermon, "The Excellency of Christ," *Works*, 4:185.

[16]Jonathan Edwards, *Treatise on Grace* in *Selections from the Unpublished Writings of Jonathan Edwards,* ed., Alexander Grosart (Edinburgh: 1865), p. 36.

[17]Ibid., p. 43.

[18]*Miscellanies,* no. 94.

[19]Ibid., no. 94.

[20]Ibid., no. 383.

[21]Perry Miller, "Ideas, Sense of the Heart, Spiritual Knowledge or Conviction, Faith, (*Miscellanies,* no. 782)," *Harvard Review* 41 (April 1948): 123-29.

[22]Perry Miller, ed., *Images or Shadows of Divine Things* (New Haven: Yale University Press, 1948).

[23]See John E. Smith, ed., Introduction to *A Treatise Concerning Religious Affections* (New Haven: Yale University Press, 1959), pp. 1-82. Also Claude A. Smith, "Jonathan Edwards and the Way of Ideas," *Harvard Theological Review* 59 (January 1966): 153-73.

[24]*Miscellanies,* no. 259. A useful discussion of Edwards on the trinity may be found in Herbert W. Richardson, "The Glory of God in the Theology of Jonathan Edwards: A Study in the Doctrine of the Trinity" (Ph.D. dissertation, Harvard University, 1963).

[25]See H. Shelton Smith, *Changing Conceptions of Original Sin,* (New York: Scribners, 1955); Dorus P. Rudisill, "The Doctrine of the Atonement in Jonathan Edwards and His successors" (Ph.D. dissertation, Duke University, 1945).

[26]For biographical information on Bellamy, see Franklin B. Dexter, *Biographical Sketches of the Graduates of Yale College* (New York: 1885), First Series; William B. Sprague, *Annals of the American Pulpit* (New York: 1852), 1:404-407, *DAB,* 2:165; and a *Memoir* by Rev. Tyron Edwards in *The Works of Joseph Bellamy* (Boston: 1850), vol. I.

[27]Joseph Bellamy, *True Religion Delineated*; or *Experimental Religion, as Distinguished from Formality on the one hand, and Enthusiasm in the other, set in a Scriptural and Rational Light, in Two Discourses,* in *Works* 1:296.

[28]Ibid., p. 295-96.

[29]Ibid., p. 368.

[30]Joseph Bellamy, "A Treatise on the Divinity of Christ," *Works, 2:473.*

[31]Ibid., p. 465.

[32]Joseph Bellamy, "An Essay on the Nature and Glory of the Gospel," *Works,* 2:334.

[33]Ibid., p. 334.

[34]For biographical information on Hopkins, see Sprague, *Annals,* 1:428; *DAB,* 9:217; Edwards A. Park, "The Life of Samuel Hopkins" in *Works of Samuel Hopkins* (Boston:

1854), vol. 1; Dick Lucas Van Halsema, "Samuel Hopkins: New England Calvinist," (Ph.D. dissertation, Union Theological Seminary, 1956); Hugh H. Knapp, "Samuel Hopkins and the New Divinity," (Ph.D. dissertation, University of Wisconsin, 1971); Joseph A. Conforti, "Samuel Hopkins and the New Divinity Movement: A Study in the Transformation of Puritan Theology and the New England Social Order," (Ph.D. dissertation, Brown University, 1975); Joseph A. Conforti, "Samuel Hopkins and the New Divinity: Theology, Ethics and Social Reform in Eighteenth-Century New England," *The William and Mary Quarterly*, ser. 3, 4, 34 (October 1977): 572-89.

[35]Samuel Hopkins, *Systems of Doctrines*, ed. (Boston: 1811), p. ii.

[36]Ibid., p. 82.

[37]Ibid., p. 82.

[38]Ibid., p. 82.

[39]Ibid., p. 83.

[40]Ibid., p. 315.

[41]Ibid., p. 350.

[42]Ibid., p. 356.

[43]Ibid., pp. 358-59.

[44]Ibid., pp. 368-69.

[45]George P. Fisher, ed., *An Unpublished Essay of Edwards on the Trinity* (New York: Chas. Scribners, 1903), p. xiii.

[46]Hopkins, *System of Doctrines*, p. 377.

[47]Ibid., p. 387.

[48]Biographical information on Emmons may be found in Sprague, *Annals*, 1:293; *DAB*, 6:150; a *Memoir* by Jacob Ide in *Works of Nathanael Emmons* (Boston: 1842), vol. 1; Emmons, *Autobiography* in *Works*, vol. 1; and Edward A. Park, *A Memoir of Nathanael Emmons, with Sketches of his Friends and Pupils* (Boston: 1861).

[49]Nathanael Emmons, *Works*, 1:34.

[50]Ibid., p. 35.

[51]Emmons, *Works*, 4:115.

[52]Ibid., p. 110.

[53]Ibid., pp. 122-23.

[54]Ibid., p. 114.

[55]Ibid., p. 95.

[56]Ibid., p. 99.

Notes to Chapter 2

[1]Thomas Emlyn, *An Humble Inquiry into the Scripture Account of Jesus Christ, or a Short Argument Concerning His Deity and Glory, According to the Gospel*, 5th ed. (Boston: 1756), p. 18. Helpful background material is contained in C. Conrad Wright, *The Beginnings of Unitarianism in America* (Boston: Beacon Press, 1955), especially chapter 9, pp. 200-22; Earl Morse Wilbur, *A History of Unitarianism in Transylvania, England and America* (Boston: Beacon Press, 1945), vol. 2, especially chaps. 20, 21, pp. 379-434; George Willis Cooke, *Unitarianism in America: A History of Its Origin and Development* (Boston: American Unitarian Association, 1902). It is by no means assumed that the major figures examined here were part of a common and single clerical establishment in New Endland. Mention has been made of Anglicans, to which could be added Separatists (many of whom became Baptists), Quakers, Methodists, and others. However, within a tolerable range of doctrinal differences, most ministers in New England served in churches organized according to congregational or independent ecclesiastical polity. As doctrinal divisions began to take on more premanent institutional forms, denominational self-consciousness and patterns of organization emerged. This development occurs late in the period under discussion, in the 1840s or 1850s. Thus, what we have referred to as the orthodox or Calvinist clergy within Congregationalism forced the liberals, or Unitarians, to organize themselves as a separate denomination.

[2]Arron Burr, *The Supreme Deity of our Lord Christ Maintained* (Boston: 1757), p. 22 Burr was Jonathan Edwards' son-in-law.

[3]Caleb Alexander, *The Real Deity of Christ, to which are added Strictures on Extracts from Mr. Emlyn's Humble Inquiry* (Boston: 1791), p. 42.

[4]John Sherman, *One God in One Person Only and Jesus Christ a Being Distinct from God, Dependent Upon Him for His Existence and His Various Powers; Maintained and Defended* (Worcester: 1805), p. 173. Sherman also leveled a blast at trinitarian usage of the terms person and being:

> To use the term persons means a distinct intellectual and moral power, a distinction of being means a distinction of persons and vice verse. Except in the case of God for Trinitarians, who hold that this is not true of Deity. The plain English of this is 'We acknowledge, that our doctrine is not true. We use words without ideas' (p. 189).

Jonathan Mayhew is representative of an anti-Trinitarianism that began to spread in the mid-eighteenth century. In a sermon on the "Nature and Principles of Evangelical Obedience," Mayhew reminded his congregation of "the unity and the supreme glory and dominion of God the FATHER: The not sufficiently preserving of which *unity* and supremacy amongst Christians, has long been a just matter of reproach to them" (*Sermons* [Boston: 1755], p. 267).

[5]Thomas Belsham, *American Unitarianism with a Preface by Jedidiah Morse*, (Boston: 1815); pp. 39-42.

[6]Jedidiah Morse, "Review of Belsham's American Unitarianism," *Panoplist* (March 1815), p. 1. This is traced more fully in James K. Morse, *Jedidiah Morse: Champion of New England Orthodoxy* (New York: Columbia University Press, 1939).

[7]Morse, "Review of Belsham's American Unitarianism," p. 11.

[8]Ibid., p. 27.

[9]William Ellery Channing, *A Letter to Rev. Samuel C. Thacher, on the Aspersions Contained in a Late Number of the Panoplist, on the Ministry of Boston and Vicinity* (Boston: 1815), p. 7. See also Samuel Cooper Thacher, "The Unity of God," (Worcester: 1817), where it is argued that the trinity is a doctrine not connected with anything essential to the Christian faith or hope.

[10]Channing, *A Letter to Rev. Samuel C. Thacher*, p. 13.

[11]Ibid., pp. 15-16.

[12]Ibid., p. 20.

[13]Ibid., p. 26.

[14]Samuel Worcester, *Letter to Rev. William E. Channing, on the Subject of Unitarianism* (Boston: 1815), p. 35.

[15]William E. Channing, *Remarks on the Rev. Dr. Worcester's Letter to Mr. Channing on American Unitarianism* (Boston: 1815), p. 20.

[16]Ibid., p. 24.

[17]Channing, "Note of First Letter," p. 7.

[18]Samuel Worcester, *A Second Letter to Rev. William E. Channing on the Subject of Unitarianism* (Boston: 1815), p. 30.

[19]William E. Channing, *Remarks on the Rev. Dr. Worcester's Second Letter to Mr. Channing or The Review of American Unitarianism in a late Panoplist* (Boston: 1815), p. 13.

[20]Ibid., p. 14.

[21]Ibid., p. 22.

[22]Ibid., p. 22.

[23]Samuel Worcester, *Third Letter to Rev. William E. Channing on the Subject of Unitarianism* (Boston: 1815), p. 17.

[24]Ibid., p. 34.

[25]Noah Worcester, *Bible News of Father, Son and Holy Ghost, in a Series of Letters in Four Parts* (Concord: 1810), p. 14.

[26]Ibid., p. 34. This was indeed the case, for the issue of the Sonship of Christ had important consequences not only for the doctrine of the trinity but for the doctrine of the atonement.

[27]Ibid., p. 86.

[28]Ibid., p. 88.

[29]Ibid., p. 174.

[30]Thomas Andros, *Bible News of the Father, Son, and Holy Ghost, as Reported by Rev. N. Worcester, A.M., Not Correct, in a Letter to a friend inclined to credit that news* (Boston: 1813), p. 27.

[31]Arron Kinne, *An Essay on the Sonship of Jesus Christ, with remarks on the Bible News by N. Worcester, A.M.* (Boston: 1814), p. 8.

[32]Ibid., p. 26.

[33]William Ware, *The Antiquity and Revival of Unitarian Christianity,* (Boston: 1813), p. 7.

[34]Thomas Worcester, *A New Chain of Plain Argument Deemed Conclusive Against Trinitarianism* (Boston: 1817), p. 42.

[35]William Ellery Channing, "Unitarian Christianity, Discourse at the Ordination of the Rev. Jared Sparks, at Baltimore, May 5, 1819," *Works* (Boston: 1893), pp. 376-90.

[36]*DAB*: 4:7. See also David P. Edsell, *William Ellery Channing: An Intellectual Portrait* (Boston: Beacon Press, 1955); Robert L. Patterson, *The Philosophy of William Ellery Channing* (New York: Bookman Associates 1952); George Park Fisher, "Channing as Philosopher and Theologian," *Discussions in History and Theology* (New York: 1880), pp. 253-85; Herbert W. Schneider, "The Intellectual Background of William Ellery Channing," *Church History* 7 (March 1938): 3-24; and a response to Schneider by C. Conrad Wright, "The Re-discovery of Channing," in *The Liberal Christians, Essays in American Unitarian History* (Boston: Beacon Press, 1970), pp. 22-40.

[37]Channing, *Works*, p. 367.

[38]Ibid., p. 371.

[39]Ibid., p. 372.

[40]Ibid., p. 372.

[41]Ibid., p. 375.

[42]Ibid., p. 375.

[43]Ibid., p. 390.

Notes to Chapter 3

[1] *The Constitution and Association Statutes of the Theological Seminary in Andover with a Sketch of its Rise and Progress* (Boston: 1808), p. 32. See also Leonard Woods, *History of Andover Theological Seminary* (Boston: 1885).

[2] For biographical information on Stuart, see *DAB*, 18:174; Sprague, *Annals*, 2:475; Edwards A. Park, *Memorial Collection of Sermons* (Boston: 1902), 179-200; John H. Giltner, "Moses Stuart, 1780-1852" (Ph.D. dissertation, Yale University, 1956).

[3] Moses Stuart, *Letters to the Rev. William E. Channing, containing Remarks on his Sermon Recently preached and published at Baltimore* (Andover: 1820); reprinted in Stuart, *Miscellanies* (Andover: 1846), p. 7.

[4] Ibid., p. 9. Jerry Wayne Brown, *The Rise of Biblical Criticism in America, 1800-1870: The New England Scholars* (Middletown, Conn.: Wesleyan University Press, 1969), is very helpful reading at this point.

[5] Stuart, *Letters to Channing*, p. 18. Stuart tried to clarify himself elsewhere by explaining that numerical unity did not preclude personal distinctions in the Godhead; the Godhead as numerical oneness with personal threeness. See Moses Stuart, "Review Reviewed," *The Quarterly Christian Spectator* 3 (August 1821); 425-35.

[6] Stuart, *Letters to Channing*, p. 21.

[7] Ibid., p. 23 Many other shared Stuart's view at this point.

[8] Ibid., p. 23.

[9] Ibid., pp. 39-40. George Park Fisher has commented:

here again, we are obliged to trace the error in part to the particular conception of the Trinity which had come to prevail in New England. Hopkins was the last to hold to the Nicene doctrine of the primacy of the Father and the eternal sonship of Christ. The whole philosophy of the Trinity, as that doctrine was conceived by its great defenders in the age of Athanasius, when the doctrine was formulated, had been set aside. It was even derided; and this chiefly for the reason that it was not studied. Professor Stuart had no smypathy with, or just appreciation of, the Nicene doctrine of the eternal generation of the Son. His conscious need of a philosophy on the subject was shown in the warm, though cautious and qualified welcome he gave to the Sabellianism of Schleiermacher. What he defended against Channing though, with vigor and learning, was the notion of three distinctions to which personal pronouns can be applied—a mode of defining the Trinity which the Nicene Fathers who framed the orthodox creed would have regarded with some astonishment. The eternal Fatherhood of God, the precedence of the Father, is as much a part of the orthodox doctrine of the Trinity as is the divinity of the son" (*Discussion in History and Theology* [New York: 1880], p. 273).

[10] Stuart, *Letters to Channing*, p. 31.

[11] Ibid., p. 188.

[12]F. D. E. Schleiermacher, *The Christian Faith*, trans. H. R. Mackintosh and J. S. Stewart (edinburgh: T. & T. Clark, 1928), par. 170.

[13]Ibid., par. 170.

[14]F. D. E. Schleiermacher, "On the Discrepancy Between the Athanasian and the Sabellain Method of Representing the Trinity," trans. with notes and illustrations by M. Stuart, *The Biblical Repository and Quarterly Observer* 18 (April 1835); p. 96.

[15]Ibid., p. 104.

[16]Ibid., p. 90.

[17]Samuel Miller, *Letters on Unitarianism addressed to Members of The First Presbyterian Church of the City of Baltimore* (Trenton: 1821), p. 90.

[18]Moses Stuart, *Letters on the Eternal Generation of the Son of God, addressed to the Rev. Samuel Miller, D.D.* (Andover: 1822), pp. 4-5.

[19]Ibid., p. 17.

[20]Ibid., p. 18. On this distinction of Son and Logos, see also Moses Stuart, "Exercitation on the Second Psalm" in *Quarterly Christian Spectator* 1 (March, 1829): 100-108; "Exegetical and Theological Examination of John 1:1-18," *Bibliotheca Sacra* 7 (January 1850): 13-53; (April 1850): 281-327; (October 1850): 696-732; and *A Commentary on the Epistle of the Hebrews* (Andover: 1860), esp. pp. 503-4, an Excursus on Hebrew 1:2.

[21]Stuart, *Letters on the Eternal Generation of the Son*, p. 77.

[22]Ibid., p. 93.

[23]Ibid., p. 110.

[24]Ibid., p. 111

[25]Ibid., p. 115.

[26]Ibid., p. 122.

[27]Ibid., p. 151.

[28]Ibid., pp. 155-56.

[29]John H. Giltner, "Moses Stuart, 1780-1852," (Ph.D. dissertation, Yale University, 1956), p. 346. See also Frank Hugh Foster, *A Genetic History of New England Theology* (New York: Russell and Russell, 1907), p. 300.

[30]For biographical material on Samuel Miller see *DAB*, 12:636; Sprague, *Annals*, 3:600; Samuel Miller, *The Life of Samuel Miller*, 2 vols. (Philadelphia: 1869); John DeWitt, "The Intellectual Life of Samuel Miller," *Princeton Theological Review* (April 1905): 168-80; Beldon C. Lane, "Democracy and the Ruling Eldership: Samuel Miller's Response to Tensions Between Clerical Power and Lay activity in Early Nineteenth Century America," (Ph.D. dissertation, Princeton Theological Seminary, 1976).

[31]Samuel Miller, *Letters on Unitarianism*, p. 11.

[32]Ibid., p. 21.

[33]Ibid., pp. 78-79.

[34]Ibid., p. 81.

[35]Ibid., p. 83.

[36]Ibid., p. 85. Special thanks are due here for the helpful suggestions of Professor H. Shelton Smith and for his editorial introductory essay to *Horace Bushnell* in the Library of Protestant Thought (New York: Oxford University Press, 1965), pp. 3-39.

[37]Miller, *Letters on Unitarianism*, pp. 192-93.

[38]John O. Nelson, "The Rise of the Princeton Theology: A Generic Study of American Presbyterianism until 1850," (Ph.D. dissertation, Yale University, 1935), p. 287.

[39]Miller, *Letters on Unitarianism*, p. 298.

[40]Samuel Miller, *Letters on the Eternal Sonship of Christ Addressed to the Rev. Professor Stuart of Andover* (Philadelphia: 1823), p. 14.

[41]Ibid., p. 16.

[42]Ibid., p. 38.

[43]Ibid., p. 47.

[44]Ibid., p. 52. Miller was a biographer of Edwards, and there are signs of the influence of the latter's thought at this point.

[45]Ibid., pp. 74-75. This same point was emphasized in James Kidd, *Dissertation on the Eternal Sonship of Christ* (Philadelphia: 1823), p. 37-40.

[46]Ibid., pp. 227-78.

[47]Samuel Miller, *A Treatise Upon the Eternal Generation of the Son, Together with Strictures upon the Letters of Moses Stuart to Channing, by an Old Soldier of the Arian War* (New York: 1821), p. 4

[48]Ibid., p. 41.

[49]Ibid., p. 41.

[50]Ibid., p. 60.

[51]Jared Sparks, *An Inquiry into the Comparative Moral Tendency of Trinitarian and Unitarian Doctrines in a series of Letters to the Rev. Dr. Miller of Princeton* (Boston: 1823), p. 133.

[52]Ibid., p. 135.

[53]Ibid., p. 180.

[54]Inevitably the trinity became tied to the moral government of God and the immoral government of man. This is nowhere more clearly stated than by the Rev. Hubbard Winslow, pastor of the Bowdoin Street Church of Boston.

> The principles of all perfect governments, whether human or divine, are essentially the same. The most perfect human governments include three distinct departments, legislative, judicial, executive. This has led many to suppose that something similar exists in the divine government, and the Scriptures certainly countenance the idea; although they do not instruct us very explicitly, or gratify our curiosity very bountifully on this subject (idem, *Discourse on the Nature, Evidence and Moral Value of the Doctrine of the Trinity*, p. 7).

The moral government of the Father, the providential government of the Son, and the sanctifying power of the Holy Spirit have an analogy in the tripartite divisions of democracy—if God rules by a trinity, so can man.

Notes to Chapter 4

[1]For biographical information on Andrew Norton, see "Biographical Notion of Mr. Norton" by William Newell, in Andrews Norton, *A Statement of Reasons for not Believing the Doctrines of Trinitarians, Concerning the Nature of God and the Person of Christ* (Boston: 1880), pp. x-1. See also *DAB*, 13:568; Sprague, *Annals*, 8:430; A.P. Peabody, *Harvard Reminiscences* (Boston: 1888), pp. 73-78. Helpful material is also in *The Unitarian Conscience: Harvard Moral Philosophy* (1805-1861), by Daniel Walker Howe (Cambridge: Harvard University Press, 1970). Conrad Wright has made a perceptive observation:

> for a number of reasons, a kind of division of labor has been established, so that one group of scholars has explored the deistic or rationalistic tradition in American religion, while a different group has dealt with the various manifestations of evangelical religion. Thus the two halves of the century have been treated in isolation; or at best, the historians of each tradition have merely used the other as a sort of foil against which their own story might most effectively be told. (idem, *The Liberal Christians: Essays on American Unitarian History p. 2).*

This same "division of labor" persists into the nineteenth century.

[2]Andrews Norton, "Review of Stuart's Letters to Channing," *The Christian Disciple* 1 (July-August 1819), p. 316.

[3]Ibid., p. 324.

[4]Andrews Norton, Preface to *A Statement of Reasons*, pp. 1-36. The Rev. Daniel K. Whitaker echoed the sentiment of Norton's *Preface* when he asserted that the truths of Christianity are clear and plain, that the love of mystery is no credit to religion. It is a diminution of revelation to act and believe "as though Christianity is an extravagant, mysterious and inexplicable system." (idem, *The Unity and Supremacy of God the Father*, p. 27).

[5]Ibid., p. 55

[6]Ibid., p. 63.

[7]Ibid., p. 152.

[8]Ibid., pp. 169-70.

[9]Brown, *The Rise of Biblical Criticism in America*, p. 70.

[10]For biographical information on Timothy Dwight, see *DAB*, 5:573; Sprague's *Annals*, 2:152; see also Stephen E. Berk, *Calvinism vs. Democracy; Timothy Dwight and the Origins of American Evangelical Orthodoxy* (Hamden, Conn.: Anchor Books, 1974).

[11]Timothy Dwight, *Theology Explained* (New York: 1851), 2:394.

[12]Ibid., p. 382.

[13]Ibid., p. 8.

[14]Ibid., p. 8.

[15]Ibid., p. 9.

[16]Ibid., p. 11.

[17]See *DAB*, 18:338; Sprague, *Annals*, 1:467; Sidney Earl Mead, *Nathaniel W. Taylor (1786-1858); A Connecticut Liberal* (Chicago: University of Chicago Press, 1942); Roland Bainton, *Yale and the Ministry* (New York: Harper and Row, 1958); Earl A.Pope, "The Rise of the New Haven Theology," *Journal of Presbyterian History*44 (March 1966): 22-44; (June 1966): 105-21.

[18]Leonard Woods (1774-1854) was among the most able defenders of Calvinism and in his nearly four decades of teaching at Andover left a deep impression on his numerous students through his lectures which were collected later into four volumes of *Works*. His discussion of the trinity provided an occasion to warn students against the dangers of mixing philosophy with faith, an error into which systematic theology fell early in its career. The simple purity of New Testament faith became corrupted by philosophical speculation about the trinity. A particularly clear and irksome instance of philosophy's intrusion upon faith is the doctrine of eternal generation. "It is, I must think, totally inconsistent and self-contradictory to say, that God eternally produced a Son, or eternally imparted personality to him, or that he eternally caused anything to take place, or anything to be which before was not, either to himself or out of himself" *(Works* [Boston: 1851], 1:440). The importance of the Sonship of Christ is reflected in the number of lectures which Woods devoted to the subject. He carefully explained to his students that Sonship was not a literal but a metaphorical designation, and "it must be remembered that metaphors have as real a meaning as a literal language. . . .(*Works*, 1:400). The errors of literalism are as great as the dangers of analogical reasoning about the trinity, especially among Unitarians who argue that nothing like a trinity of persons in the Godhead can be found among created beings and therefore conclude that there can be no trinity in God. The truth is, "this thirst for analogy forsakes revelation, for Christ's relation to the Father has no real and strict analogy either in his person or his office" (*Works*, 1:275). There are real personalities and genuine personal relations in the Godhead, but describing these in terms of human analogies breaks down. In short, it is best simply to accept the trinity in faith and not think too much about it.

[19]Nathaniel W. Taylor, *Essays, Lectures, Etc., Upon Select Topics in Revealed Theology* (New York: 1859), p. 1.

17855

[20]Ibid., p. 16.

[21]Ibid., pp. 33-34.

[22]Ibid., p. 92. See Sydney E. Ahlstrom, "The Scottish Philosophy and American Theology," *Church History*:24 (September 1955) 257-72.

[23]Ibid., p. 96.

[24]Ibid., p. 104.

[25]Ibid., p. 108. Taylor's essay on the trinity breaks off abruptly, and one suspects it was left unfinished. The Christological implications of Taylor's doctrine of the trinity may be traced in part in Nathaniel W. Taylor, "Notes on Revealed Theology," taken by R. C. Learned, 1838-1840, Taylor papers, Library of Yale Divinity School, New Haven, Conn. He was thoroughly unsympathetic with the doctrine of eternal generation.

Notes to Chapter 5

[1]The best source of biographical information is the *Life and Letters of Horace Bushnell* (New York, 1880) by his duaghter, Mary Bushnell Cheney. See also Barbara M. Cross, *Horace Bushnell: Minister to a Changing America* (Chicago: University of Chicago Press, 1958); Theodore T. Munger, *Horace Bushnell: Preacher and Theologian* (Boston: 1899); *DAB*, 3:350. For Bushnell on the trinity, see especially William A. Johnson, *Nature and the Supernatural in the Theology of Horace Bushnell* (Lund, 1963), pp. 143-65. On Bushnell's theory of language, see Donald A. Crosby, *Horace Bushnell's Theory of Language in the Context of Other Nineteenth Century Philosophies of Language* (The Hague: Mouton, 1975), especially chap. 6, "Language and the Trinity: Three Views," where Crosby presents a perceptive discussion of Andrews Norton, Nathaniel W. Taylor, and Bushnell.

[2]Josiah W. Gibbs, *Philological Studies with English Illustrations*, quoted in Smith, ed., *Horace Bushnell*, pp. 36-37. A further discussion of Bushnell on language and theology may be found in C. Conrad Cherry, "the Structure of Organic Thining: Horace Bushnell's Approach to Language, Nature and Nation," *Journal of the American Academy of Religion*, 40 (March 1972); 3-20.

[3]Horace Bushnell, "Revelation," an address delivered before the Porter Rhetorical Society of Andover Seminary, September 3, 1839, Bushnell Papers Yale Divinity School Libary, New Haven, Conn. The closing paragraphs of this address are published in Horace Bushnell, *The Spirit in Man* (New York: 1910), pp. 357-59.

[4]Ibid., n.p.

[5]Cheney, *Life and Letters of Horace Bushnell*, p. 90.

[6]Ibid., p. 192.

[7]Horace Bushnell, *God in Christ* (Hartford: 1849), pp. 25-26.

[8]Ibid., p. 30.

[9]Ibid., p. 45.

[10]Ibid., p. 48.

[11]Horace Bushnell, "Concio ad Clerum: A Discourse on the Divinity of Christ; Delivered at the Annual Commencement of Yale College, August 15, 1848," *God in Christ* p. 122. The full discourse is reprinted in Smith, ed., *Horace Bushnell*, pp. 152-96.

[12]Ibid., p. 131.

[13]Ibid., pp. 135-35.

[14]Ibid., p. 137.

[15]Smith, ed., *Horace Bushnell*, p. 34.

[16]Bushnell, *God in Christ*, p. 140.

[17]Ibid., pp. 147-48.

[18]Ibid., p. 151.

[19]Ibid., p. 175.

[20]In a letter dated March 10, 1851, Bushnell wrote that *Christ in Theology* was "less interesting than the other, because it is less free and less of a simple outspeaking of myself. But as a discussion of points, it is far more adequate than the other. . .Ths volume has cost me five times the labor which the other cost, because it has put me to the investigation of others, which to me, is the hardest and most difficult of all sorts of work" (Cheney, *Life and Letters*, p. 246). George P. Fisher wrote that "he [Bushnell] was indisposed to patient scholarly investigaton" and studied primarily for purposes of self-defense. See George P. Fisher, "Horace Bushnell," *International Review* 10 (January 1881): 13-25.

[21]Horace Bushnell, *Christ in Theology: Being the Answer of the Author, before the Hartford Central Association of Ministers, October, 1849, for the Doctrines of the Book entitled "God in Christ"* (Hartford: 1851), p. 12. A brief account of the main developments of the controversy surrounding Bushnell, see Smith, ed., *Horace Bushnell*, pp. 152-59.

[22]Bushnell, *Christ in Theology*, pp. 12-13.

[23]Ibid., p. 23.

[24]Ibid., p. 92.

[25]Ibid., p. 130.

[26]Ibid., p. 137.

[27]Ibid., pp. 172-73.

[28]Ibid., p. 170.

[29]Ibid., p. 172.

[30]Ibid., p. 172.

[31]Ibid., p. 187.

[32]Ibid., p. 184.

[33]Ibid., p. 176.

[34]Horace Bushnell, "The Christian Trinity a Practical Truth," *New Englander* 12 (1854): 488-89.

[35]Ibid., pp. 491-92.

[36]Ibid., pp. 496-97.

[37]Ibid., p. 497.

[38]Fred Kirchenmann, "Horace Bushnell: Orthodox or Sabellian?" *Church History* 33 (March 1964): 58; see also Smith, *Horace Bushnell,* p. 198.

[39]Bushnell, "The Christian Trinity, a Practical Truth," pp. 501-2.

[40]Horace Bushnell, "Our Gospel a Gift to the Imagination," in *Building Eras in Religion* (New York: 1881), 275-87.

[41]Ibid., 259-60.

[42]Horace Bushnell, "Our Relations to Christ in the Future Life," in *Sermons on Living Subjects* (New York: 1883), p. 42. Donald Crosby has overlooked this important sermon in his discussion of Bushnell on the trinity, an oversight that removes some of the strength of his criticisms of Bushnell. See Crosby, *Horace Bushnell's Theory of Language,* pp. 222-24.

[43]Ibid., p. 452.

[44]Ibid., p. 461.

[45]Ibid., p. 463.